Suc KU-524-890

Fuchsias

WITHDRAWN

REINHARD HEINKE

Series Editor:
LESLEY YOUNG

MEREHURST

Contents

4 **Introduction**

6 **All about fuchsias**

6 A brief history of fuchsias
6 Where do fuchsias originate?
6 The development of hybrids
6 New varieties through mutation
6 The difference between cultivating fuchsias and creating new cultivars
7 How the wide range of colours was created
8 American fuchsias
8 The classification of fuchsias
8 Nomenclature
8 Species and varieties
8 The parts of the fuchsia flower
9 Classifying fuchsias
9 Colour descriptions in catalogues
9 Foliage
10 Shape and growth
11 Seeds and fruit

11 **Tips on buying fuchsias**

11 Ideal growing sites
11 Positions to avoid
11 Improving sites
12 Protection from the wind
12 Shade
12 Improving humidity outdoors
12 Improving humidity indoors
13 Choosing fuchsias for particular sites
13 Fuchsias for the patio or balcony
13 Fuchsias for the garden
13 Fuchsias and sun tolerance
14 Hardy fuchsias
14 Fuchsias for the greenhouse or conservatory
14 Fuchsias for indoors
14 Where to buy your fuchsias
15 Points to consider when buying fuchsias

"Joy Patmore" is ideal for training into a standard.

16 Transportation and initial care

17 **Successful care and training of fuchsias**

17 Suitable containers
17 Soil
17 The pH factor
18 Mixing your own potting compost
18 Buying potting compost
18 Improving the soil in your garden
18 Feeding
19 Essential nutrients
19 Initial feeding
19 Regular feeding
20 Planting fuchsias in containers
20 The correct spacing of plants
20 Planting fuchsias in flowerbeds
20 Watering
20 How often to water
22 Using the right water
22 Automatic watering
22 Fully automatic irrigation
22 Clipping and pruning
23 Repotting
23 Fuchsias in hydroculture
24 Training fuchsias
24 Bush and shrub shapes
25 Plants for hanging baskets
25 Standard fuchsias
25 Pyramids
25 Espaliers
25 Bonsai
26 Grafting

Contents

26 **Pests and diseases**

26 Preventive measures
26 Methods of control
28 Physiological damage
28 Waterlogging
28 Salt damage
28 Drying out
28 Damage from sunlight
28 Mechanical damage
29 Symptoms of nutrient deficiency
29 Fungal attack
29 Mildew
29 Rust
29 Grey mould
29 Physiological disorders
29 Pythium: root rot
29 Pests
29 Vine weevils
30 Caterpillars
31 Red spider mites
31 White fly
31 Cyclamen mites
31 Aphids
31 Thrips
31 Protection of indoor plants
31 Helpful insects
31 Herbal brews

32 **Propagating fuchsias**

32 Propagating methods
32 Propagating equipment
32 Propagating using cuttings
33 Caring for cuttings
33 Pricking out and potting on
34 Repotting
34 Propagating by layering
34 Propagating with underground
   shoots

34 **Overwintering without
   problems**

34 Feeding
34 Watering
34 Moving bedding fuchsias
34 Pruning for overwintering
35 Positions for overwintering
35 Overwintering above ground or
   in earth pits
37 Overwintering in composting
   pits
37 Subterranean greenhouses
37 Light shafts
37 Outside cellar steps
37 Dark cellars
37 Attics and lofts
37 Indoors
37 Conservatories
37 Greenhouses
37 Using electric lighting
38 Care of dormant plants
38 Cutting back in the spring
38 The fuchsia year
39 How to prune
39 Care after cutting back
39 Watering after dormancy
39 Feeding after dormancy
40 Repotting
40 Gentle pruning
40 The right position
40 Fuchsias in the greenhouse
41 Protecting plants in the
   greenhouse

41 Early flowering without a
   greenhouse

43 **A selection of exquisite
   fuchsias**

43 Key terms
43 Varieties/cultivars and species
60 Useful information
60 International fuchsia societies
60 Preparing fuchsias for an
   exhibition or show
60 Hybridizing

62 **Index**

Fuchsia speciosa in flower.

"Annabel" needs a shady position.

Introduction

Names like "ballerina flower" or "bell flower" have often been used to describe the appearance of the enchanting fuchsia flower. Fuchsia flowerheads conjure up images of graceful dancers in delicate petal skirts, or rippling wind chimes, ringing gently at the slightest stirring of a breeze. Since their discovery nearly 300 years ago, fuchsias have charmed many a gardener and plant lover with their incomparable beauty. Nowadays, fuchsias are very popular indeed and you will hardly ever find a garden, patio or terrace without at least one of these delightful plants. Increasing international travel and a passion for collecting among keen gardeners have both contributed towards the trend for new varieties to be imported worldwide and for old ones to be rediscovered.

More often than not, the very first fuchsia to be bought is a luxuriant hanging variety with large flowerheads in vibrant colours, which promises to be an eyecatching feature. Once bitten by the bug, however, the fuchsia enthusiast soon becomes fascinated by the details of smaller-flowering varieties and begins to cast a covetous eye on varieties with bizarre flower shapes - in short, he or she has begun to discover the endless range of beautiful hybrids.

This colourful guide will introduce you to many examples from the fascinating range of fuchsia varieties and cultivars.

The author, Reinhard Heinke, an experienced professional gardener and fuchsia specialist, gives advice on the successful care of fuchsias in the garden or indoors, on a patio or balcony, in a greenhouse or conservatory. His instructions and tips are easy to understand and can be followed by any keen amateur. Even readers with little gardening experience will find his explanations simple to follow and will soon be able to grow fuchsias with healthy foliage and luxuriant blooms.

You will learn what points to look for when buying fuchsias and about the best positions in which to keep them, but also how a less-suitable site can be improved to make conditions better for your fuchsia plants. The author, Reinhard Heinke, who has cultivated countless fuchsia species and varieties in his nursery in Dortmund, Germany, and who communicates frequently with fuchsia lovers and specialists, uses his own practical experience of growing fuchsias to explain how to plant, water, feed and prune them, so that your plants will continue to bloom in all their splendour year after year. He gives advice on suitable overwintering conditions and on how to prune correctly in order to obtain the particular plant shape you are aiming for and to coax your plants to produce the maximum amount of flowers. Step-by-step colour illustrations are also used to impart practical gardening skills.

Information on pests and diseases, as well as tips on their control through traditional methods, is given together with advice about successful preventive measures, biological control and plant protection. You will also find out how easy it is to propagate fuchsias and how to try your hand at hybridizing. Glorious colour photographs, taken especially for this guide, and showing some of the most beautiful fuchsia cultivars, convey only an impression of the magnificent beauty and diverse range of fuchsias. A special chapter, that describes and illustrates both well-known and new cultivars and varieties, will help you to pick your favourite individual plants for the garden or patio. Even longstanding and experienced fuchsia lovers are sure to find something new among this selection.

The author

Reinhard Heinke is a professional nurseryman who has successfully cultivated and hybridized fuchsias for many years.
He is the author of numerous reports and papers on the subject.

Acknowledgements

The author and publishers wish to thank all those who contributed towards the making of this volume, especially Friedrich Strauss for the exceptionally beautiful photographs, and Ushi Dorner for the excellent and informative illustrations.

A group of fuchsias
Several upright, semi-hanging and trailing varieties planted in tubs and well set off by two luxuriantly blooming standards, "Beacon" (left) and "Deutsche Perle" (right).

All about fuchsias

Fuchsias were originally discovered by a French priest, were named after a German botanist, first hybridized by British gardeners and were perfected by French, German and American gardeners. For almost 300 years the fuchsia has intrigued plant lovers all over the world. There are currently over 100 species and close to 10,000 varieties.

A brief history of fuchsias

The first fuchsia was probably discovered around 1695. A French botanist named Father Charles Plumier (1646-1704) came across fuchsias during his third expedition to South America, while on the island of Santo Domingo. He described the plant in his book *Nova Plantarum Americanum Genera*, published in 1703, as a delicate flowering shrub, and named it *Fuchsia triphylla flore coccinea* (which means "three-leaved fuchsia with red flowers") in honour of the well-known German botanist, Leonhart Fuchs (1500-66). According to Linnaeus's nomenclature, it is classified as *Fuchsia triphylla*. During the period from 1768 to 1840, further species were discovered, all of which were introduced to Britain. From 1836 to 1843, the German botanist K. T. Hartweg was commissioned by the British Royal Horticultural Society to collect fuchsias in Central America.

Where do fuchsias originate?

The natural area of distribution of fuchsias stretches for thousands of miles, beginning on the islands around Haiti and Santo Domingo and spreading southward from Mexico and Central America to Patagonia at the tip of South America. It is a curious fact that fuchsias only seem to occur naturally along west coasts, with one exception: in a limited area, west of Rio de Janeiro (on the east coast of the American continent), where some species have become naturally established. A few species are also to be found on Tahiti and in New Zealand. After the fuchsia had been introduced to Europe, *magellanica* strains soon spread along the western coasts of the British Isles, growing even in Scotland and Ireland. Although fuchsias are at home in tropical regions, they cannot really be described as typically tropical plants. They grow mainly on lightly wooded mountain slopes up to 3,000 m (about 9,850 ft) where humidity is very high and the soil is rich in humus, well aerated and well drained.

The development of hybrids

A hybrid plant is created by the crossing of two different, pure-species parents. This can take place through wind or insect pollination or by human interference. At the time of writing, scientists are engaged in research that is attempting to establish whether species that exist in their countries of origin, such as *Fuchsia magellanica*, or *Fuchsia bacillaris*, were produced by natural hybridization. The first hybrids to be created by people appeared from 1832 onwards, through the crossing of different varieties, with *Fuchsia magellanica* as one of the parents. Other growers crossed already existing wild varieties to create new hybrids.

New varieties through mutation

Pollination by wind or insects (new varieties), or by human agency (new cultivars), can create new fuchsias. However, other factors, known as mutations, can also change the general picture. These are characterized by the sudden appearance of variations in the colours of flowers or leaves or in their growth. The changes are caused by such triggers as environmental shock due to a change of climate, radiation or the influence of cellular toxins, such as colchicine, derived from the autumn crocus. More recently, radiation and toxins have been purposely used in order to cause mutations. Cuttings are then taken from any parts of the plants showing alterations and are allowed to root, thus creating a new cultivar.

The difference between cultivating fuchsias and creating new cultivars

People who grow plants are often said to be raising plants when, in fact, they only grow or cultivate them. A genuine raiser or hybridizer is someone who crosses two chosen parent plants so that a new variety or cultivar will be created, which he or she alone has the right to name.

Popular varieties: (from left to right) "Charming", "Joy Patmore", "Deutsche Perle", "Lady Isobel Barnet".

How the wide range of colours was created

One of the most beautiful and most appreciated characteristics of fuchsias is the range of colours, including multi-coloured varieties, all of which have tended to inspire hybridizers to experiment:

● Orange – one of the fuchsia species first discovered, *Fuchsia triphylla.*
● Violet – *Fuchsia lycioides* and *Fuchsia arborescens.*
● Whitish-green combined with red – *Fuchsia excorticata* and *per-scandens.*

● Bright pink – *Fuchsia microphylla.*
● Flame red – *Fuchsia fulgens.*
Yellow-orange – *Fuchsia splendens.*
● Whitish-green with reddish-orange – *Fuchsia denticulata.*
The above-named species were among the first to be used for hybridizing, especially in Britain. In 1840, the first cultivar was created with a white tube, white sepals and a purple corolla. It was named "Venus Victrix" and was later used for numerous further crossings. Many plants that now bear flowers with white parts contain genetic material from this cultivar. A cultivar

with a pure white corolla was first successfully created in 1848. This meant that the main colours for further combinations were now secured. Around the turn of the century, the number of new cultivars in Britain decreased. Instead, French and German hybridizers began to produce new cultivars, which are still to be found in the range of available varieties. In Germany, the raising of *tryphilla* hybrids became very popular. These sun-resistant varieties, bearing flowers in racemes, are now grown all over the world.

American fuchsias

Fuchsia lovers convened in California in 1929 to found the first society in the world dedicated to the study of fuchsias, the American Fuchsia Society. In 1937, one of the first results of hybridizing was exhibited. A new trend in hybridizing, producing hybrids with very large flowers, was imminent. Brilliant glowing colours and new flower shapes were created. Many of these American hybrids became the forerunners of a new wave of fuchsias in Europe.

Then, in the 1970s, another wave of exciting hybrids hit the fuchsia market. Although it was generally accepted that the range of fuchsia colours had already been exhausted, a number of new varieties now appeared, bearing flowers with a dark aubergine-coloured corolla and sky-blue stamens. Their names were "Amke", "Foolke" and "Foline".

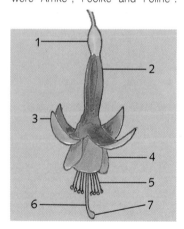

The parts of a fuchsia flower
1 ovary
2 tube
3 sepals
4 corolla (petals)
5 stamen (filaments and anthers)
6 style
7 stigma

The classification of fuchsias

The fuchsia has its own place within the botanical classification system. It belongs to:
- the division of *Angiospermae;*
- the class of *Dycotyledons;*
- the order of *Myrtales;*
- and the family, or natural order of *Onagraceae.*

It is closely related to the indigenous willowherb *(Epilobium)*, to the yellow-flowering common evening primrose *(Oenothera biennis)*, *Godetia* and *Clarkia.*

Nomenclature

The naming of fuchsia species and varieties has been firmly established and is thus internationally applicable and comprehensible. Naming is regulated by the "International Code of Nomenclature for Cultivated Plants". Those readers who know a bit of Latin may be able to derive some information about the country of origin and characteristics of a plant from its botanical name, which is made up of two or more parts, for example, *Fuchsia boliviana var. luxurians alba.*

Fuchsia is the genus name; *boliviana* is the species name which indicates Bolivia as the country of origin;

var. luxurians, when translated, means "luxuriant variety" – *var.* is the abbreviation for *variegata;* alba is Latin for "white".

The last part of the name describes the colour of the variety which developed naturally in the wild. In this example, it deviates from the original red *Fuchsia boliviana var. luxurians.*

Subspecies are designated with the abbreviation ssp., for example, *Fuchsia bacillaris ssp. bacillaris.* Bastard species, which are crosses within the same species, are described thus: *Fuchsia x bacillaris.*

Hybrids are created by crossing two different species within the same genus. The result is no longer homozygous (species-pure). The garden fuchsia is called *Fuchsia hybrida.*

Cultivars are the "offspring" of crosses between different species or different existing cultivars, for example, *Fuchsia hybrida* "Kwintett".

Species and varieties

While no exact figures exist, according to some estimates there are probably about 10,000 varieties worldwide. As no totally comprehensive classification books exist for fuchsias, one still has to resort to checking the illustrations or photographs in specialist volumes. More recently, sheets of photographs, intended for identification purposes, have appeared sporadically, but these do not pretend to be complete either. The number of fuchsia species still flourishing in their natural state in the wild is estimated at over 300.

The parts of the fuchsia flower

An illustration of the parts of a typical fuchsia flower is shown left. The flower comprises:
- the tube;
- the sepals;
- the petals or corolla;
- the male stamens, consisting of the filaments and the anthers;
- the female ovary and the stigma and style.

Various flower shapes are a further, distinguishing feature of different fuchsias (see illustration on p. 9), for example, single, semi-double and double flowers.

Depending on the species or variety, the sepals and corolla will appear in various shapes, the flowerbuds may be slim, longish or spherical.

Classifying fuchsias

It is almost impossible to classify fuchsias or to compare them with each other by using colour descriptions alone. In order to make a proper identification, it will be necessary to consider the shape of the flowers, of the fuchsia's growth and of the leaves, the shape of the ovary, the length and shape of the tube, the shape, length and positioning of the sepals, the shape and positioning of the corolla, the length of the style and stigma and the colouring of the stamens. In most international literature on fuchsias, the colours of the flowers have usually been translated directly or equivalently from English. What is really missing so far is some kind of good colour grading, including subtler nuances, that is accurate, clear and definitive. However, it is also true to say that, in the case of fuchsias, it is not an easy task to give exact descriptions of colour. Almost every fuchsia lover will confirm that the flowers may change colour subtly due to varying growth conditions. Their colours are dependent on:
● whether planted outside in beds or containers;
● the type of soil and soil composition (peaty, clay, acid, neutral or alkaline soil);
● the age of the plant;
● the electrostatic properties of the plant cells, depending on the amount of moisture in the soil;
● feeding;
● the site (bedded out or in a greenhouse);
● position (exposed, shady, sunlight or artificial light);
● the weather during the time when the flowers are developing.

RHS colour classification

More recently, raisers of fuchsias have adhered to the colour classification system established by the RHS (Royal Horticultural Society,

The shapes of flowers

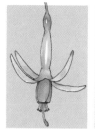

There are three types of flower shape, depending on the number of petals (corolla). Left: single (four petals), variety "Mrs Lovell Swisher". Centre: semi-double (seven petals), variety "Margaret". Right: double (more than seven petals), variety "Moonraker".

Britain). A system of letters and number combinations gives clues when determining the colours. However, even these should be used with caution as the colour values only apply exactly to a flower at a particular moment of maturity.

Colour descriptions in catalogues

In catalogues and lists of varieties, the first-mentioned colour always refers to the outer petals or sepals of the flower and the second colour to the corolla. Checklists give detailed information on the colour of:
● the tube;
● the sepals, in detail, from the base to the tips and, if necessary, the outer and inner surfaces;
● the corolla, from the base to the edges;
● the style and the stigma;
● the anthers and filaments.
Usually, there are also indications as to the shape of the ovary (see illustration, p. 8).

Foliage

To a large extent, the outer appearance of a flowering plant is determined by its foliage. Leaves may enhance the beauty of the flower or, alternatively, may even subdue it.

The shape of the leaves may vary considerably from one fuchsia species to another. Among hybrids the most common are:
● medium green to dark green, longish, elliptical leaves with a serrated edge, as seen in the most commonly available varieties;
● the slightly velvety, smoother-edged, longish leaf of the *tryphilla* hybrids.
On the other hand, the leaves of some wild species or varieties may not appear at all typical of fuchsias. For example:
● in whorls, in formations of three or four, shiny, with slightly hairy edges, as in *Fuchsia magdalenae*;
● fernlike and delicate, as in *Fuchsia microphylla*;
● green on top with a silvery underside, as in *Fuchsia excorticata*;
● egg-shaped and matt, as in *Fuchsia procumbens*;
● smooth-edged and shiny, as in *Fuchsia arborescens*;
● shiny dark green with a light green underside as in *Fuchsia denticulata*;
● velvety, large-surfaced and light green, as in *Fuchsia fulgens*.
The colours of the leaves may range from light to dark green and even reddish. There are also several mutations which are whitish-green, yellow-green, white-red-green, yellow-red-green, and yellow.

Shape and growth

It is only possible to estimate the probable future development of a particular fuchsia while it is still a young plant that is growing naturally. If the plants have been interfered with, stunted through the use of chemicals, had their tips pinched out, been staked or been positioned too close together, it is usually no longer possible to give an opinion. Such factors as lack of water, too much sunlight, fertilizing with too much phosphorus or a lack of trace elements can also result in stunted growth. Fuchsias can be differentiated by their various types of growth, which can make an individual plant especially suitable for training into a particular shape (for example, bush type, hanging type, standard, and so on, see p. 24). Common types are:

● the upright kind, which grows vigorously;
● the many-shooted, compact growing or rather low growing type;
● the hanging type with vigorous growth;
● types that hang elegantly and have many soft shoots.

Seeds and fruit

The size of fuchsia fruits depends on the species and individual cultivar. They can look rather like sloes or even cherries. The fruit ranges in colour from green to reddish to almost black. It is fleshy and contains seeds in four compartments. The number of seeds may vary considerably. It is worth noting that not all varieties are capable of producing seeds that will ripen to the point where they can propagate. Generally speaking, fuchsia fruits are edible, but vary greatly in taste. British fuchsia lovers have been known to produce wine, preserves and chutney from the ripe fruit. The fruit can also be made into a delicious fuchsia fruit flan.

"Arcadia" will flourish in hanging baskets in a semi-sunny position.

10

My tip: The fruits taste best if you pick them when they are completely ripe. Dark fruits taste better and have more flavour than light-coloured ones. They taste a little like cherries. Wash the fruits well, remove the stalks and slice.

Recipe for fuchsia preserve

● Ingredients: 900 g (2 lb) ripe berries, 900 g (2 lb) preserving sugar, citric acid.
● Method: Extract the juice from the berries, stir the juice with the preserving sugar and citric acid and boil for ten minutes.

Recipe for fuchsia flan

● Ingredients for the dough: 225 g (8 oz) flour, 1 tsp baking powder, 50 g (2 oz) sugar, 100 g (4 oz) butter, 2 beaten egg yolks, 2 tbsp water.
● Ingredients for the fruit layer: 450-900 g (1-2 lb) sliced fuchsia fruits, 2 tsp thickening (corn starch), ¼ tsp cinnamon, ⅛ tsp grated nutmeg, 2 tbsp sugar.
● Method: Sift the flour and rub in the chopped butter. Mix in the sugar. Make a well in the centre and add the eggs and water and mix to a dough. Knead the dough until smooth. Leave in refrigerator for half an hour. Grease a flan dish and press the dough into it. Spread the fuchsia fruit on top. Bake in the oven at 200°C (392°F) 30-40 minutes, until the edge of the pastry is golden brown and the fruit is soft.

Recipe for a fuchsia dessert sauce

● Ingredients: 900 g (2 lb) fuchsia fruits (finely sliced), 50 g (2 oz) sugar, 1 tsp corn starch, 1½ tbsp lemon juice, ¼ tsp each of cinnamon and ground cloves.
● Method: Allow the ingredients to simmer gently in a covered pan until the fruit is very soft. Stir lightly and serve warm or cold with ice-cream or custard.

Tips on buying fuchsias

Fuchsias are prized for their prolific flowering habit in half-sunny to shady positions, whether in the garden, on patios or terraces, on balconies or in window boxes. There are winter-flowering varieties, sun-loving species and varieties and even hardy fuchsias. All will flourish without a great deal of care, as long as they are positioned correctly. Even if the site is not ideal, a few simple improvements are often all that is needed to do the trick.

Ideal growing sites

Fuchsias are natural forest dwellers. In their countries of origin, they grow on humus-rich, well-drained soils and are permanently surrounded by fresh air, high humidity and gentle, filtered light. If you are able to simulate these conditions to a reasonable degree, you will always be lucky with your fuchsias. The best positions are:
● patios or balconies facing east to receive morning sunlight;
● south-west, west or north-facing positions with afternoon or evening sun;
● south-facing gardens that are not in direct sunlight all day long;
● flowerbeds on the east or west side of the house;
● beds that are half-shaded or include shade-providing, taller, neighbouring plants;
● north-facing positions, but only if the plants have permanent, unimpeded access to light.
Never put fuchsias in a position that is too dark. They will grow there but will bear only a few flowers.

Positions to avoid

Unsuitable sites will visibly affect the growth and general well-being of fuchsias. Such positions encourage disease and pests, promote unnatural growth and result in sparse foliage and falling leaves. The following sites are most unsuitable for fuchsias:
● hot positions with dry, still air;
● draughty patios or balconies;
● badly ventilated rooms.
Even the sun-loving *triphylla* hybrids will not manage without a good supply of humid air and reasonably moist soil.

Improving sites

For those who are really determined to grow fuchsias, we can provide a few tips on how to improve sites that offer less than favourable conditions. This advice may help to supply plants with the environment they require. Often the answer is simply a matter of small adjustments which may benefit neighbouring plants as well.

Protection from the wind

Fuchsias like airy surroundings but not if they are too draughty. In a strong wind there will be a tendency for the plants' young shoots to break off. Therefore, if your patio or balcony is too windy or the fuchsia's position against the house wall is too draughty, some form of windbreak should be erected, such as:
● porous cladding or opaque matting;
● trellises or open fencing, thickly covered by climbing plants;
● a group of neighbouring plants or bushes which will break the force of gusts of wind or protect the fuchsias from draughts.

In a flowerbed, fuchsias will be well protected from the wind if they are planted between broad evergreen plants of varying heights, which will offer protection from strong gusts of wind. Mixed beds of bushes, shrubs and standard plants of various heights will afford mutual protection.

Shade

Shade is especially important if you plan to cultivate varieties that are very sensitive to direct sunlight, or if you have only a very sunny spot for your plants. Fuchsias kept in a conservatory that lacks shade, or in a small greenhouse, will require adequate shading, such as:
● trellises with bushy climbing plants or creepers;
● synthetic shading mats for greenhouse plants (affix the mats to the outside of the greenhouse!);
● UV protection screens, venetian blinds or awnings for the conservatory.

Important: If you are growing fuchsias on a window ledge, you must begin to protect the young plants from the midday sun from the middle of spring onwards. Pull down the blind or awning between noon and 3 pm or cover the plants with sheets of tissue paper or a thin, semi-transparent cloth.

Improving humidity outdoors

This is not absolutely essential for fuchsias that are in a semi-shaded position outside and are watered regularly, the exception being in summertime when there are long periods of high pressure.

In less favourable positions, improving the micro-climate around your plants is recommended, as follows:
● daily spraying with water in morning and evening but never in full sunlight as leaves and flowers may become burnt;
● a humidity-dispensing source in the immediate vicinity; for example, water running over rocks, a fountain, a small pool or a basin of water;
● neighbouring plants with large leaves that lose a lot of water through evaporation (and will also require a lot of watering);
● low-growing, spreading plants that will prevent the soil from drying out (for bedding fuchsias and standards);
● a 5-cm (2 in) layer of mulch, made of grass cuttings, chopped straw, rotting compost or bark (for bedding fuchsias), to prevent the soil from drying out.

My tip: Sow seeds or plant low-level lobelia under your standard fuchsias in mid-spring. The lobelia will soon produce a thick, slightly overhanging carpet of blue flowers, which will not only harmonize well with the many colours of your fuchsias but will also keep the soil moist for longer.

Improving humidity indoors

Follow these tips to produce flourishing fuchsias in your greenhouse or conservatory or indoors:

In the greenhouse : In the mornings on hot summer days, use a water spray to create a fine mist around your plants. Afterwards, allow plenty of fresh air to blow through. In this way, you can supply humidity and cool air to encourage evaporation all in one go.

Fuchsias for small patios and balconies

Upright fuchsias

Name of cultivar	Colour of flower (sepals/corolla)
"Happy"	red/blue-violet
"Lady Thumb"	red-white/pink-veined
"Larissa"	white/pink
"Minirose"	white/red-violet
"Robert Stolz"	red/purple
"Tom Thumb"	red/purple-violet

Hanging fuchsias

"Elfriede Ott"	old rose/dark pink
"Harry Gray"	white/white
"La Campanella"	white with pink blush/ purple-violet
"Lisi"	white/violet
"Postiljon"	white with green tips/ violet
"Wiebke Becker"	white

Young fuchsia plants need spraying daily, in the mornings, after you have placed the plants on a 2-3-cm (½-1 in) layer of sand or on a capillary mat, both of which must be kept moist at all times.

In the conservatory spray the plants with water every day, to provide a fine water mist.

Indoors you should also spray your fuchsias every day to raise the humidity. Further possibilities are to:
● stand shallow dishes of water in between your fuchsia pots;
● pack peat moss into the space between the plant pot (must be made of clay) and the outer pot and keep the peat moist;
● stand the plant pots on a dish containing sand or Hortag, which must be kept moist at all times.

Important: Indoor plants that have been sprayed with water will rarely dry out as fast as those outside. Do not leave spraying until the evening, as the flowers and leaves should be dry when they enter their rest phase at night.

My tip: Always use soft water for spraying, to avoid the appearance of unsightly, chalky-white deposits on the leaves and flowers.

Choosing fuchsias for particular sites

If you happen to fall in love with an unknown fuchsia on a market stall or in a flower shop, you do not need to be a botanist to figure out what position the plant would prefer. By its very appearance, the plant will "tell" you, at a glance. *It is generally true to say* that the larger the surface of the leaf, the softer it is, and the larger and many-petalled the flower, the shadier the site should be during the summer. White-flowering varieties may discolour, turning pink in too much sunlight.

Fuchsias for the patio or balcony

The range of plants from which to choose is quite breathtaking. When buying, do not be tempted just by beautiful flowers but take note of the shape in which the plant is growing. This will tell you something about what container to use for it.

Upright varieties with vigorous growth look best when planted separately in large containers.

Plants with many shoots, growing compactly and tending to stay low, are best in low, wide containers and tubs.

Plants with hanging branches and vigorous growth are good for hanging baskets.

Elegantly trailing types with lots of soft shoots are suitable for tubs, free-standing urns, pedestals and smaller hanging baskets.

My tip: If you have only a small balcony, choose varieties that will not tend to spread out too much (see table, p. 12).

Fuchsias for the garden

You will truly be inspired by the enormous range of varieties that is available (pp. 43-59). Whether you decide on a bed of fuchsias only or on a mixture of plants, the choice is limitless. Combinations of standards and bush fuchsias will create diversity and offer mutual protection. If you combine fuchsias with shrubs or summer flowers, however, or plant them in front of trees, you will need a little skill and some knowledge of the varieties. With their idiosyncratic shapes and multi-coloured flowers, fuchsias can be rather dominating. Neighbouring plants in soothing shades of green, conifers, deciduous trees, grasses and quiet expanses of lawn are less competitive and create a suitable background. Shrubs of one colour only and summer flowers in shades of pink, blue and white will accentuate the vibrant colours of the fuchsia flowers.

Fuchsias and sun tolerance

Fuchsias that can tolerate sunlight

Characteristics	Fuchsia cultivars
Fuchsias flowering in racemes with slightly hairy and often reddish leaves.	"Thalia", "Koralle", "Göttingen" "Elfriede Ott"'
Fuchsias with leathery, narrow leaves, and many small flowers	"Happy", "Little Beauty", "Tom Thumb", "Liebreiz"
Fuchsias with orange flowers.	"Groenekan's Glorie", "Walz", "Parasol", "Orange Flare", "Chang",
Hanging or upright cultivars with medium sized flowers.	"Achievement", "Joy Patmore", "La Campanella" "Lisi", "Kwintett"

Fuchsias that cannot tolerate much sun

White flowers	"Flying Cloud", "Sleigh Bells", "Annabel", "Ann H. Tripp"

My tip: When planning your garden, remember that, as a rule, fuchsias are not hardy plants. Position your fuchsias in such a way that they will be easy to dig out in the autumn for transferring to winter quarters (see p. 34).

Hardy fuchsias

These charming bushy fuchsias will fit in beautifully among shrubs or rows of trees and can cope with a lot of sun, as long as you maintain "cool feet" by mulching underneath. Their flowering time begins in mid-summer and will last until the first frosts arrive. While these fuchsias do better in a maritime climate and will hardly deteriorate at all in winter, areas with a dry-cold, temperate winter climate will cause them to behave just like other shrubs: the parts above the ground will die down. In the spring, the roots will put out new shoots. In warm, sunny positions, depending on species and varieties, the plants may reach heights of up to 1.5 m (5 ft).

My tip: Plant hardy fuchsias 5 cm (2 in) deeper than usual and use frost protection, just as for roses, from the first month of winter onwards.

Fuchsias for the greenhouse or conservatory

In summer or winter fuchsias will only do well in a greenhouse if you can make sure the temperature is right. For overwintering (see p. 34), 5°C (41°F) will be sufficient, but for young plants you will need 15°C (59°F) or more. If you long for winter flowering fuchsias, you could try some of the *triphylla* hybrids or *Fuchsia speciosa*, *Fuchsia arborescens*, "First Success" or "Miep Aalhuizen". Ideal temperatures are 15°C (59°F) in the daytime and 8-10°C (46-50°F) at night.

Fuchsias for indoors

Keeping fuchsias as house plants is not entirely without its problems. Living conditions inside houses have changed so dramatically over the last few decades that fuchsias purchased when in flower tend to look beautiful for only a few days before the leaves and buds begin to drop. The reason for this is that the plant requires fresh air, a natural drop in temperature at night and humidity of at least 70%. Those who have rooms with the older style of non-insulated, slightly draughty windows, may try growing the smaller-flowered varieties until they come into bud.

Where to buy your fuchsias

The range of plants on the market has never been as varied as it is now, all thanks to enthusiastic fuchsia raisers and gardeners, collectors and dedicated fuchsia lovers, who have formed clubs and societies (see p. 60), and are continually acquiring and importing new, exciting varieties. As they are not all suitable for mass cultivation, you should choose carefully and buy from a variety of sources, especially if you are not content with the most popular, easily available varieties.

Flower shops: During the main planting period, from the end of spring into early summer, your local florist will probably stock suitable bedding plants and varieties for patios or balconies, as well as choice individual plants. He or she may be able to replenish the stock daily and should be able to supply plants quickly if they are ordered.

Nurseries: In most areas there should be at least one nursery that grows young fuchsia plants and will have them available at various stages of growth. As a rule, the nursery staff should have a fairly large range of varieties and should

be in a position to advise you. You will be able to take your plants away immediately, expertly packed in suitable containers, with instructions on care supplied.

Garden centres: They are in a position to offer large quantities of plants at reasonable prices. However, the range of varieties will depend on their selling policies. You will hardly ever find any botanical rareties here, but you will probably be able to save money on the purchase of large quantities of popular varieties for bedding out. Another advantage is that you will also find a huge selection of plant containers, soils and potting composts, plant protection agents and literature.

Mail order: This method of purchase is good if you are buying a few choice, or especially unusual, varieties. As the plants have to be mailed before flowering time, you will be able to order them from very early in the spring until the middle of spring.

These young plants will then grow on under your tender care until they reach a plantable size (towards late spring) and are ready to flower.

Specialist nurseries with a mail order service: These firms, usually run by fuchsia lovers and collectors, are generally restricted to dealing with fuchsias only, and are therefore in a position to offer a choice of 300-1,500 varieties. The plants are dispatched unpruned, with a root stock that is 5-8 cm (2-3 in) long, and, depending on the variety, will be 5-20 cm (2-8 in) high. These plants are especially suited for training into a standard or being grown as a solitary plant. Mailing time is from early spring to early summer.

In addition, there is the possibility of visiting specialist nurseries right through until autumn, and purchasing there directly.

"Checkerboard"

"Gartenmeister Bonstedt"

"Brutus"

"Royal Velvet"

"Covergirl"

"Petit Point"

Regional shows: This is where private collectors and fuchsia enthusiasts exhibit their favourite plants. You will find enchantingly lovely and rare varieties here and will be able to chat about fuchsias to your heart's content and exchange notes with other dedicated fuchsia lovers.

When to buy your fuchsias
At the end of spring, after the usual cold spell has passed, is the time to start planting fuchsias outside. If you are growing individual plants, or wish to plant fuchsias earlier in containers, you should be able to obtain well-established young plants even earlier than this. In the house, make sure to keep them in a light, but cool and airy position.

Points to consider when buying fuchsias

Choosing healthy plants
A healthy appearance is a prerequisite for good growth and the development of plenty of flowers:
● look for vibrant colours and shiny, perfect leaves, spaced not too far apart;

● spotty leaves, especially ones near the stem, are a sign of fungal infection;
● check the undersides of the leaves, where pests like white fly might be lurking;
● the plant should display compact growth;
● the tips of the shoots should be full of buds;
● roots should be firm and white.

In the foreground, the variety "Texas Longhorn"; in the background "Happy".

"Ullswater" is named after the romantic Lake District in England.

Note the description of the variety. This will give you some indication of its origins, the colours of the flowers and its use. Very often, there is additional valuable information on how to protect your plant, along with tips on care. Unfortunately, it is usually only specialist varieties that come equipped with all this information. In the case of popular mass varieties, you will have to ask about the name, characteristics, potential height of the plant and colours of the variety offered for sale.

Transportation and initial care

The best way to transport fuchsias is on pallets or in flat boxes, packed closely together. Hanging fuchsias are best wrapped separately in large sheets of newspaper. This way, they can be transported lying down. All fuchsias, including those that arrive by mail order, should be unpacked very carefully and left to stand in boxes in a shady place to recover. Gently spraying them with water will quickly revive wilting shoots. After two to three days you may move the fuchsias or plant them but do not put them outside until after the last cold snap of late spring. Should grey mould have formed inside the packing, treat the plants with fungicide (see p. 29) and stand them in a dry place, not too close together and well protected from wind and sun.

My tip: Fuchsias need to have fresh air circulating around them. Never leave them in closed rooms, as the plants will quickly lose their leaves and buds.

Successful care and training of fuchsias

Plant them, water them, feed them and spare the time for a bit of beauty care – fuchsias are not a lot of work if you know what to do and what they like. If you enjoy training and shaping fuchsias, you can use the summer months to turn young plants into luxuriant bushes, picturesque standards, pyramids, trellis plants or bonsai.

Suitable containers

If you do not wish to plant your fuchsias in beds, you will need to choose containers carefully. Fuchsia plants' height and individual characteristics will dictate their rate of growth and readiness to flower, as will the type of soil or potting compost chosen.

Most important prerequisites: drainage holes. Fuchsias cannot stand waterlogging. Also, make sure the tub or container is not too small – at least 20 cm (8 in) deep and the same width.

Wooden containers will give your fuchsias a rustic air but the wood should be treated five months in advance with a plant-friendly wood preservative. To prevent the wooden floor of the container from rotting, it is best to stand the container on two thick wood offcuts or on a couple of bricks, or to use the special clay-pot feet that are obtainable at garden centres. This will enable air to circulate underneath the container.

Clay containers, made of terracotta, majolica, or ceramic, for example, not only look especially decorative but their considerable weight will provide good stability so that they will not tip over easily. The disadvantage is that they may develop a chalky bloom on the outside wall (except for glazed ceramic), and also break easily. There is also a tendency for plants to dry out quickly in these containers.

Industrially manufactured containers, such as those made of asbestos-free cement or fibreglass, do not tip over and are durable.

Plastic containers are easy to clean, obtainable in all sizes and colours and weigh very little (important when moving plants in the autumn). They should be doublewalled, so that they will not heat up too quickly in hot sunlight, which could damage the roots.

The disadvantage is that plastic containers are often not stable as they are so light in weight. You must remember that a fully grown standard fuchsia needs anchoring if it is to be left in an exposed position on a patio or high balcony.

Containers made of copper or brass are suitable but should be clad on the inside with a tough layer of foil, otherwise they will oxidize.

Make sure water can drain away!

My tip: When using very large, deep containers, first place a layer of sand or gravel in the bottom, before filling with potting compost. This will help to anchor the fuchsias.

Soil

The right soil is very important for fuchsias and the correct potting compost is vital if you are using containers as then the plants have to make do with a limited amount of soil and the roots cannot develop as freely as in a flowerbed.

A good potting compost should be just like good garden soil: friable, to let air circulate, containing plenty of humus and well drained but also able to retain moisture. It should be a well-balanced mixture of organic and inorganic substances.

The following components should be present:
● coarse, not too mature, light moss peat;
● fine, well-matured, dark sedge peat;
● well decomposed, three-year-old garden compost;
● bark humus;
● coarse sand or other substances to prevent waterlogging, and keep the soil loose, such as polystyrene granules, Perlite or Hortag.

The pH factor

The pH factor is an indicator of soil acidity. Fuchsias thrive on slightly acid to neutral soil with a pH factor somewhere between 6 and 7. If they grow in soil that is too acid or too alkaline, many of the necessary nutrients become inaccessible to their roots. You can measure the pH factor with a strip of litmus paper (obtainable at most chemists) or with a pH meter (obtainable through garden centres etc.).

Planting in a larger pot or container

Cover the drainage hole with a piece of broken pot, then cover this with 2-3 cm (½-1 in) drainage layer of gravel or pot shards. Fill in enough soil or compost so that the fuchsia is sitting at the same depth as in the last pot. Leave 2 cm (½ in) at the top for watering. Fill in the rest of the soil and press down. Insert a stick for support.

As a rule, peat is too acid. Moss peat, for example, has a pH factor of 4-4.5, while sedge peat registers below 4. In order to neutralize moss peat, mix in 3-3.5 g of lime per litre (2 pt) of damp peat; for sedge peat use double the amount of lime.

Mixing your own potting compost
Some gardeners like to prepare their own compost. The following are some examples of tried and tested mixtures.
Recipe 1
1 part garden soil (clay soil with humus)
2 parts moss peat
¹/₁₀ part lime-free river sand (obtainable from builders' merchants)
3-3.5 g lime per litre (2 pt) of soil
1.5-3 g concentrated fertilizer per litre (2 pt) of soil or use long-lasting fertilizer and follow the manufacturer's instructions.
Recipe 2
6 parts potting compost
2 parts clay
10 parts peat
1½ parts sand
1½-3 g concentrated fertilizer or long-lasting fertilizer per litre (2 pt) of soil
3-3.5 g lime per litre (2 pt) of soil.

My tip: Both mixtures can be improved by adding Hortag, polystyrene granules or Perlite (up to 2%). Mixtures containing little garden soil or compost should be mixed with a micro-nourishing fertilizer, in amounts of 10g per 100 litres (22 gal) of soil.

Buying potting compost
Among the commercially produced types of compost there are cheaper kinds, which usually consist of dark sedge peat, and more expensive types of gardener's compost, which contain light moss peat, dark sedge peat, clay, bark humus and aerating substances, such as polystyrene granules or sand.
The following types of commercially available, ready-mixed composts should be available from your local garden centre or nursery and are worth recommending:
● compost specially intended for rooted cuttings and young plants;
● composts for use when planting in boxes and containers;
● composts containing long-lasting fertilizer, for use when planting in containers.

Improving the soil in your garden

Poor garden soils can be improved by adding humus, nourishing substances and aerating materials.
Lime-rich soils (pH factor over 7) can be neutralized by working in peat.
Acid soils (pH factor under 5.5) are balanced by mixing in lime or crushed limestone.
Sandy soils that are poor in nutrients and too well drained can be enriched with well-rotted manure, peat or bark humus. To ensure better water-retaining properties, mix in hygro-mulch.
Medium heavy clay soils can be improved by adding peat, rotted manure and bark humus. For better aeration, work in polystyrene granules.
Heavy clay soils must be drained to avoid waterlogging. For this purpose, dig the soil over a good 20 cm (8 in) deeper than normal and make it looser by adding peat, manure or bark humus. Coarse sand, Perlite or Hortag will provide permanent drainage qualities.

Feeding

Like all profusely flowering, vigorously growing plants, fuchsias require regular and sufficient feeding.

The three golden rules of feeding plants:
● Feed only during the growing period, from spring to late summer. Then, gradually stop feeding altogether, so that the woody parts can mature.
● It is preferable to feed little and often, rather than to give a high-concentration dose.
● Never feed on to dry soil nor in full sunlight.

My tip: In kitchenware shops you can buy measuring spoons in various sizes. These can be quite useful for measuring out low doses of plant food.

Essential nutrients

Almost every bag of fertilizer will display the three magic letters: NPK! N stands for nitrogen, P for phosphorus and K (kalium) for potassium. These are the three main ingredients in every concentrated fertilizer. In addition, fuchsias also need other minerals and a few trace elements: calcium, sulphur, iron, molybdenum, magnesium, boron, manganese and zinc. The main nutrients, NPK, are contained in various concentrations in fertilizers, for example: NPK 14:10:14 means that this fertilizer contains 14 parts N (nitrogen), 10 parts P (phosphorus) and 14 parts K (potassium). This would be the correct nutrient ratio, for example, during the main growing period. The right choice of fertilizer to give to a plant depends on its stage of growth at that particular time.

For growth of leaves and shoots in spring, the plant will require a fertilizer with more nitrogen and potassium and less phosphorus.

For the development of buds and flowers in the summer the proportions of phosphorus and potassium should be higher than in spring.

For maturing wood in the late summer potassium especially is needed.

NB: Shoots that have not yet formed roots should not be fertilized.

Initial feeding

This is intended as a starter boost. Mix the fertilizer into the soil or compost before planting.

In the case of *bedding fuchsias*, this first feed may consist of long-lasting fertilizer (use a dosage as prescribed on the package) or 100 g (3½ oz) of concentrated mineral fertilizer (plus 150 g or 5¼ oz lime for acid soil) per square metre (sq yd). If you prefer concentrated organic fertilizer, choose one with a high potassium/magnesium content and work in 150-200 g (5¼-7 oz) per square metre (sq yd).

For fuchsias in containers (it does not matter whether you have chosen pots, tubs or urns), enrich the potting compost with a long-lasting fertilizer. The fertilizer granules will release nutrients steadily over at least a ten-week period (follow the dosing instructions on the packet carefully).

My tip: If you use an organic fertilizer, make sure to check that it

Supporting a hanging plant
Varieties that hang flat over the edge of the pot will become more attractive if a few shoots are tied up or if the central shoots are supported.

contains an appropriate amount of potassium/magnesium, as, without these, the plants may become overfed and lazy to flower. If you prefer a mild, nitrogen-based, long-lasting fertilizer, try working coarse hoof and bone meal into the ground. When using a mineral-based, long-lasting fertilizer, you should check its period of effectiveness, which can last from three to nine months.

Regular feeding

Feeding should begin when the fertilizer that was first mixed in with the potting compost has almost been used up, which is after about one to three months. It can be done in various ways:

● Using a mineral fertilizer dissolved in water. Do not use more than 2 g or 2 ml per litre (2 pt) of water, and fertilize twice a week during the main growing period. When the buds begin to form, fertilizing once a week will be sufficient.
● Sprinkling on organic fertilizers, mineral fertilizers or long-lasting fertilizers.

Create bushy growth and more flowers by removing shoot tips

As soon as three sets of leaves have formed, pinch out the topmost set. Buds will begin to sprout in the leaf axils and side shoots will begin to develop. Again, after three sets of leaves have appeared, pinch out the shoot tip. Fuchsias flower at the tips of shoots.

● Feeding the leaves. Plants with weak or diseased roots can also be fed through their leaves. If necessary, spray daily with 1.5‰ solutions (that is, 15 ml fertilizer to 10 litres or 2½ gal of water).

Planting fuchsias in containers

Before starting, prepare your equipment carefully:
● Soak new containers thoroughly in water, so that any toxic substances are washed out and the pot can take in and drain off water.
● Used pots should be well scrubbed, rinsed with clean water and dried in the sun.

How to plant (illustration, p. 18):
● Cover the drainage hole with a piece of broken pot.
● In the case of very large, deep containers insert a drainage plate, or fill the base with Hortag, pot shards or gravel. Over this layer place a thin mat of interfacing fabric, cambric, linen, or something similar, so that the drainage layer does not become clogged with compost.
● Cut off any damaged shoots, shorten shoots that are too long and remove all dead or withered parts.
● Scoop some of the potting compost into the pot. (If it is very dry, moisten it.) Set the fuchsia plant on top of this. The stem adjoining the root system should not sit any deeper in the soil than it did in its previous pot.
● Fill in the soil evenly around the plant and press it down gently. Leave a gap for watering of about 1-2 cm (up to ½ in) from the top edge of the pot.
● Water thoroughly.
● Support taller plants with a plastic-coated steel rod or with a bamboo cane.

The correct spacing of plants
Depending on the shape in which the plant is growing and the characteristics of this particular variety, you may have to space them far apart or plant them close together. In general, leave a space of 25-35 cm (10-14 in) between plants. Basically, the root stock will need several inches of fresh soil around it. *In small hanging baskets* (about 15 cm or 6 in in diameter) use only one plant; in larger baskets (from 25 cm or 10 in in diameter) you can plant three fuchsias.
For large containers choose luxuriantly growing varieties, such as "Checkerboard", "Celia Smedley", "Kwintett", "Charming", "Groenekan's Glorie", "Billy Green" and "Göttingen".

Planting fuchsias in flowerbeds

After first moistening the root stocks, plant the fuchsias in prepared soil, at the same depth as they were previously planted in their pots. Press down gently, leaving a "gulley" around the stem, and water thoroughly twice, using the sprinkler attachment on your watering can. Then cover the "gulley" with dry earth. For solitary plants, do the following:
● Plant straight into the flowerbed. Advantages: the fuchsia will have a lot of room around its roots, need not be watered so often and will become strong and healthy. Disadvantage: for overwintering (see p. 34), the fuchsias will have to be dug up and repotted, which is not so easy if the root system is well developed.
● Plant in a container and sink it into the ground. Adavantage: the fuchsia can be dug up with the container for overwintering. This will save unpotting and repotting again later on. Disadvantage: there is less room for the roots to spread out.

● Put the plants in wire or plastic baskets and plant these. Advantages: roots may grow through the lattice or weave and take advantage of nutrients and water. The fuchsia can be dug up together with the basket, for overwintering, and placed in a large pot – this will save repotting.

Watering

The frequency and quantity of watering will depend on several factors.

The basic rules for watering fuchsias:
● Give them a good soaking. Do not just wet the surface;
● During the spring and autumn, water in the mornings so that the foliage is dry by the evening;
● Always pour away any surplus water in the dishes or bowls underneath the pot – waterlogging is bad for fuchsias.
Remember also that where plants are growing close together, almost no rainwater will penetrate through the leaves to reach the soil. Regularly test the soil underneath by poking it with a finger to check whether it feels moist. When the temperature changes from cool and rainy to dry and sunny, plants may go limp rather quickly, even when the root system is still moist. The plants will need some shade so that they can recover.

How often to water
Bedding fuchsias only need extra watering during long dry spells. Use a sprinkler, which should be kept going long enough to saturate the soil to a depth of at least 10 cm (4 in).

A beautiful hanging plant
A true "flower ballet" performed by "Cecile", a hybrid hanging fuchsia created in the USA in 1981.

Solitary plants with especially large root stocks need extra watering, even when planted in a bed. If the area around the roots looks lighter in colour than the surrounding soil, the plant needs water.

Standards often receive too little rainwater because of their wide, spreading heads, so they will need frequent extra watering!

Fuchsias in pots, tubs and containers will need regular daily watering during the summer.

Baskets should be watered in the morning and evening on hot days. If the soil becomes so dry that it is shrinking away from the edge of the container, then the plant should be lifted down and immersed in water until the root stock is completely soaked.

My tip: Tie up baskets on a pulley system, so that the basket can be lowered easily for watering. This system will also make it easier to deadhead and care for the plant.

Using the right water

Rainwater is ideal but do not collect it if it has just rained for the first time after a long dry period, as it will then contain too many harmful substances!

Mains water is fine for fuchsias, as long as it is not too hard or too cold when used on the plants. If it is over 13 degrees Clark (ask the water supply company, or your parish council), you will need to soften the water. For values between 3 and 19½ degrees Clark, suspend a small sack containing 200 g (7 oz) of peat in a 10-litre (2½ gal) watering can overnight. Renew the peat after it has been used three times. If the chalk content (hardness) is even higher, mix a chemical water softener with the water (obtainable from garden centres etc.).

The quality of **well or spring water** can vary greatly and it is not always good for plants. Only use it for

watering if you have used it successfully before.

Automatic watering

This is an ideal solution for people who have limited time in which to care for their plants, and also while you are on holiday. The simplest systems work on the principle of capillary action. If the soil is dry, water-sensitive clay cones, fibreglass wicks or mats will soak up water from a reservoir.

Important: If you intend to go away for an extended period, you should test beforehand whether the quantity of water in the reservoir will be sufficient!

Other "plant sitters" are:

● Boxes with built in water reservoirs. They will work without a hitch as long as the containers are under cover and the water-sensitizing system is not interfered with from above by rain falling into it.

● The "gardener's box". This innovation, designed by experts, provides the fuchsias with a water supply of 12 litres (2.6 gal) per square metre (sq yd) of box.

● A hydroponic system can be installed quite easily inside existing

containers and consists of containers that are equipped with drainage holes in the second third of the container, leaving the bottom third as a water reservoir. The entire container is filled with Hortag and the root stock placed in it. The clay pellets will provide the roots with an adequate supply of water and oxygen. Make you sure you carry on feeding the plant regularly.

Fully automatic irrigation

The most important part of this aparatus is an electronically controlled checking system. Water-sensitive "feelers", called tensiostats, pass commands to a magnetic valve, which opens or closes the water-supply duct. This fully automated irrigation system can be installed in any kind of water distribution system, and run on showers, jets, a single stream or droplet hose. Depending on individual sizes of pots, the quantity of water supplied must be determined beforehand.

Clipping and pruning

Fuchsias flower continuously for long periods of time – sometimes

Training standard fuchsias

Left: Do not cut off the top shoot of the young plant, as it will form the head later on. Cut off the lower side shoots and flowerbuds. Let the leaves remain on the stem. Allow the plant to grow to the desired height and then prune. Centre: Cut every shoot on the head back to the first set of leaves. Right: Continue cutting off the tips of side shoots.

for over five months. If you want your fuchsia plants to look good all the time, to appear bushy and flower ceaselessly, you will have to be willing to spend some time on fuchsia beauty care.

Regular deadheading and pruning will retain the beauty of your plant and keep it healthy. Once a week, remove withered flowers, damaged parts and fruit stalks with a sharp knife or a pair of scissors. Leave the stalks of removed leaves and fruit to fall off by themselves. They will heal better that way. Avoid creating any raw surfaces through tearing the plant, as mould tends to form on these wounds rather quickly.

Pinching out or cutting off new shoots will rejuvenate the plant and encourage it to form further shoots. There is a tendency for growth to slow down after a while and for fewer flowers to form. During the early part of the flowering period, if you cut back every fourth to fifth shoot a little, every ten days or so, you will prevent the growth of long, straggly branches. Depending on the distance between sets of leaves, the shoots should be cut back to three or five sets of leaves. Each of these pruned shoots will develop three to five times as many new shoots and, in six to seven weeks, they will be full of flowers.

Cutting back in the autumn, before taking the plants inside, and again in the spring, before repotting them, are all part of the essential tasks before and after overwintering (see p. 34).

A special kind of cutting back is employed for training fuchsias as bushes, espaliers, standards or bonsai (see pp. 24-26).

My tip: Even if it is a lot of work, clear away fallen flowers and leaves under densely growing groups of plants, as this is the best prevention against grey mould (see p. 29).

Supports for standards
Left: home-made supports made out of a metal tube (anchored firmly in the soil) and fixed to the edge of the pot with "claws" and two crossed pieces of strong wire to provide support for the head.
Right: Special "tutor" plant support.

Repotting

Young fuchsias have a healthy appetite and, as a rule, use up nutrients in the soil very fast. The ideal time to repot is at the start of the growing season in the spring. However, there are other occasions.

Repot them:
● after overwintering (see p. 34);
● if the plant is not doing well (see p. 26);
● when young plants have grown especially vigorously and their roots no longer have enough room in the pots. In this case, repotting may be done but only until the beginning of the last month of summer.

Important: The diameter of the new pot should be only 2 cm (about 1 in) larger than the old pot in order to ensure fast spreading of the roots. Soil without roots in it tends to become acid and may harm the plant.

My tip: Plants that are several years old should be watered only sparingly after being cut back and repotted. If visible shoot ends do not carry on growing, remove the fuchsia from its pot and check the roots. If they are brown and rotten, remove all the bad parts from the root stock and plant the fuchsia in fresh soil.

Fuchsias in hydroculture

Generally speaking, fuchsias are well suited to this type of culture, although, in practice, the general preference seems to be for growing them in soil.

Points in favour of hydroculture are:
● easy care;
● strong, stable plants;
● good growth.

The points against are:
● late flowering;
● less willingness to flower;
● problems with overwintering;
● no good way of anchoring supports.

If you still want to try this method, grow your young shoots or cuttings in a hydroculture rooting medium (very fine Hortag pellets). Rooting will take place in pots that are wrapped in polythene bags and placed on a heated mat or in a heated germinating box. I do not recommend transferring plants from soil culture to hydroculture.

Training fuchsias

Fuchsias are a good subject for training. You can train them into various shapes and, compared with many other plants grown in containers, this can be done relatively quickly. In less than two years, you should have a decorative little tree. The only essential requirement for shaped fuchsias is young, vigorous, well-rooted plants. There are many varieties which are particularly suitable for this kind of training and shaping.

The right tools are also essential. You will need a knife, rose clippers, sticks, twine, a support for the crown of the tree, espaliers and wire.

Bush and shrub shapes
Start pinching out as soon as the main shoots are fingerlength, removing the tips of shoots together with one or two sets of leaves. This will encourage the development of many side shoots. The most suitable plants for this are bedding fuchsias that you have grown yourself.

Plants for hanging baskets
Plant these baskets using fuchsias that tend to hang down slightly and have branches that do not jut out too far. Pinch out the shoots after they have formed a fourth set of leaves. The six or eight new young shoots which appear after that should be tied up as in the illustration on p. 19. If you wish to grow plants to hang against a wall, train the shoots around the front and sides but leave the back bare. In the case of free-hanging baskets, bushiness will be obtained by gathering several branches at the centre or by cutting back one of the branches, which will then produce a lot of side shoots.

Bush fuchsia with attractive flowers – hanging variety "Daisy Bell".

Standard fuchsias

You can begin training fuchsias into the shape of bushes or standards (see illustration, p. 22) in the summer or even in spring.

Training in the summer:

● In the later part of summer, begin cutting shoots from the chosen parent fuchsia, choosing shoots that do not have just one set of leaves but, preferably, a triple set as a better, bushier head will be obtained from a stem that produces triple sets of leaves. These will form the basis for several good standards or bush shapes. Root the cuttings (see propagation, p. 32).

● Early in the autumn, replant these young plants in pots of approximately 10 cm (4 in) in diameter, drive in a support stick and tie the fuchsia to it. Pinch out young laterals and flowerbuds immediately. Do not remove any leaves.

● Preferably, the stem should be 70-80 cm (27-30 in) tall before the start of winter, to avoid uneven woodiness. Stand the young tree in a bright, but not too sunny or warm, position.

● In the second and third months of the winter season, prune the tree back to the above-mentioned height, or the height you desire, for the first time and tie the stem firmly to the support stick immediately below the head of the tree. Allow the laterals of the topmost two or three layers to grow to a length of about 20 cm (8 in), and then prune them back to the first set of leaves. Regularly remove any laterals that appear lower down on the stem but do not remove any leaves that appear immediately on the stem! The fuchsia will need these for photosynthesis.

● During the second month of spring, prune again and cut back every new lateral to the first set of leaf axils.

● After the middle of the last month of spring (following the last cold snap), you may take the young standards outside, where they will start to develop healthy shoots.

Training in spring:

● If you start at the end of winter, begin by planting a single-shooted, unpruned, young plant in a pot, support it with a stick and then regularly pinch out all laterals and buds.

● In late spring, the plant may be cut back to the height you wish. After developing new laterals, the plant may be transferred outside.

● In early summer, cut back a second time, after which allow the plant to produce flowerbuds freely.

My tip: Fuchsia shoots and other parts of the plant snap off easily. Make sure you provide the heavier head of a standard with sufficient support. One of the simplest methods is to insert a ring made of plastic-coated, 4-mm-thick wire, to which the head is tied (see illustration, p. 23). Proper plant supports made of galvanized steel are even better and can be obtained for standards at heights of 55-120 cm (about 2-4 ft) (illustration, p. 23).

Pyramids

This shape presents a bit of a challenge to the experienced fuchsia lover. The main problem is to make sure that the lower branches of the fuchsia are encouraged to go on producing shoots. If this fails, the lower third of the treelet will look bare and you will be left with no other option than to train it as a standard. Pyramids will take two or three years of training to make an ideal shape. The best place for this process is a greenhouse.

Method

Choose a profusely flowering, upright variety and find a well-rooted offshoot that has grown straight. Support it with a stick, so that the stem can grow tall and straight. Encourage the plant to produce shoots all the time. Use a support frame to coax laterals into a horizontal position. In the second year of growth, or when the fuchsia has become woody, the frame may be removed. All laterals must be grown under identical conditions. Prune back for the first time when the laterals that are longer than 20 cm (8 in) have become woody, and cut them back to the first third. This will gradually produce the desired pyramid shape. At the same time, cut back the tip, so that the newly shooting parts will be evenly distributed.

Espaliers

The sight of an espalier fuchsia can be quite breathtaking. The frame it grows against may be made of wood or plastic. Always train several plants at the same time. As soon as the main stem has reached the required height, cut the top off (illustration, p. 19). The vitality of the plant will now become concentrated in the laterals which should also have their tips removed as soon as they have grown wider than the espalier. Tie up the laterals horizontally and prune out every second set of shoots.

Bonsai

Fuchsias have a tendency to become very woody even during their first year, so they are especially suitable for training as bonsai trees (table, p. 26). Hanging varieties, such as "Multa", "Minirock" and "Postiljon" are easy to train into cascades, a special form of bonsai.

Method

Encourage the plant to branch profusely by continually pruning it back (p. 19). Begin the actual training and shaping during the second and third years. Later, cut back the new shoots to two sets of leaves. Wiring is usually not necessary with fuchsias, which have a natural tendency to grow in bizarre shapes, and it is only to be recommended if other means of shaping have failed.

My tip: If you would like to know more about bonsai shaping, consult your nearest bonsai club. Addresses can be found at your local library or at a garden centre or in the telephone directory.

Grafting
Years ago, before it was possible to train the stem of a standard to be sufficiently tall and strong within one period of growth, the method of grafting was employed. The stem base often used was the reliable "Deutsche Perle". There were various ways of grafting, all of which had their pros and cons. If you are interested in trying out different methods of grafting, it is worth approaching your nearest fuchsia society for advice and information.

Fuchsias suitable for bonsai

Name of cultivar	Colours (sepals/corolla)
"Happy"	red/blue-violet
"Hummeltje"	white-pink/light pink
"Lady Thumb"	red-white/red-veined
"Little Beauty	light red/lavender blue
"Lottie Hobby"	scarlet/scarlet
"Minirock"	red/red
"Tom Thumb"	pink/purple-violet
"Vielliebchen"	shining red/deep violet

Pests and diseases

Mistakes made in the care of fuchsias or the unfavourable positioning of plants can weaken even the strongest fuchsias and render them easy prey to voracious insects and destructive fungi and moulds. Fortunately, there are ways of dealing with these enemies.

Preventive measures

● make sure you buy only healthy plants with vigorous growth;
● ensure a well-aired, bright position with adequate humidity;
● do not overfeed. Too much food can lead to spongy growth;
● do not overwater; make sure the water is not too cold and water the leaves only in summer;
● avoid waterlogging at all costs;
● do not pot the plant too deeply;
● spray your plants with an infusion of mare's tail (Hippuris vulgaris). The silicic acid contained in this plant will firm up the fuchsia's tissues and make it resistant to moulds and fungi;
● keep an eye on your plants. Early diagnosis of problems will often make the need for drastic treatments unnecessary.

Warning: All plant protection agents, even biological ones, must be kept in a place that is inaccessible to children or domestic pets.
NB: In professional nurseries all plant protection agents are stored in locked cupboards and only handled by specially trained employees. Ask them for advice and, if possible, use biological preparations.

Methods of control

The main prerequisites for successful control of pests and diseases are watchfulness, perseverence and, if necessary, repeated treatment.
Remedial action can be taken by:
Chemical means – spraying or watering with pesticides and fungicides.
Mechanical means – removing infested and diseased parts of the plant and removing pests.

Salmon pink bush fuchsia
Even fuchsias that hang down can be trained into attractive bush shapes. This American cultivar is called "Orange Mirage".

Biological control – using natural predators of the pests, such as predatory mites, lacewing flies or other useful insects.

Alternatives – sticky yellow strips (for example, bio-friendly greenhouse fly catchers, obtainable in garden centres), odour traps, herbal brews and infusions, or aromatic plant sprays containing etheric oils, which are employed with great success in professional nurseries.

Physiological damage

This term describes diseases that are not caused by insects or micro-organisms but are due to mistakes made in care. The most likely systems to be upset by this are plant metabolism and water equilibrium.

Too much water will push oxygen out of the soil, make the temperature drop and encourage root rot by creating favourable conditions for soil moulds and fungi.

Too little water will result in drying out of the root stock, the correct electrostatic equilibrium within the plant tissues will be disturbed and the plant will wilt.

Too much feeding will lead to chemical burns on the roots, if there is a surplus of mineral salts, and to unnatural, unhealthy growth if too much nitrogen has been given.

Too much sunlight can cause burns and discoloration of the leaves in plants that naturally occur in a forest habitat (illustration right).

Too little light will cause the plant to look leggy and unhealthy. It will form long, pale, weak shoots, which are very susceptible to disease.

Too high a temperature will lead to falling leaves.

Too low a temperature will interfere with growth.

Waterlogging
Symptoms: Limp and falling leaves,

together with a very moist root stock and black, rotted roots.
Causes: Too much water, no proper drainage holes, soil that is packed too tightly or long periods of rain.
Remedy: Let the root stock dry out and, possibly, stand the plant under cover. In severe cases, put the plant in a smaller pot or in better-drained soil. Trim off any decayed roots beforehand, and treat the cut surfaces with charcoal powder (obtainable from garden centres).

Salt damage
Symptoms: limp leaves, pale green to transparent leaves that turn brown later. Sudden dropping of leaves that are still green.
Cause: Too much feeding too often, possibly on a dry root stock.
Remedy: Remove the plant from its pot, loosen the root stock and cut the dead roots right back to healthy tissue. Repot the plant in a smaller container filled with potting compost, water sparingly and protect from wind and sun. As soon as the roots have filled the pot, the plant may be transferred to a larger pot.

Drying out
Symptoms: Foliage that appears yellow towards the centre of the

Damage and disease .
Left: Effects of shock due to too much light.
Right: Mildew (mould).

plant, withering flowers and buds. Soil shrinking away from the edges of the pot.

Causes: Not enough water or superficial watering. The inner part of the root stock is not able to get enough water. Once it has completely dried out, water will simply run off it.
Remedy: Completely immerse the pot and the dried-out root stock in water until no more bubbles rise to the surface.
Important: Even in winter, make sure the root stock never dries out completely.

Fungal infection
Left: Rust.
Right: Grey mould.

Damage from sunlight
(Illustration left)
Symptoms: red and green patches on leaves (chlorophyll damage), burn marks on all parts above ground.
Causes: Too bright and sunny a position. "Light shock" due to sudden change of position from a roofed-over site into bright late spring sunlight.
Remedy: A build-up of red pigment, a protective measure produced by the plant against too much light, will generally disappear on its own when the fuchsia has become acclimatized. In the case of burn marks, choose a shadier position or create shade for the plant. Cut back damaged shoots as they will not recover.

Mechanical damage
Symptoms: Leaves with holes, torn leaves or snapped-off shoots.

Causes: Damage caused by the gardener's clumsiness, wind, hail or other action of the weather.
Remedy: Use a sharp knife to cut back to the healthy wood.

Symptoms of nutrient deficiency
These can often be a sign of a pH factor that is too low but this is fairly rare when using modern potting composts.
Symptoms: Pale (chlorotic) leaves indicate a lack of iron, yellow leaves with green veins indicate a lack of manganese, yellow areas and dead parts of leaves without a proper edge indicate a lack of magnesium.
Remedy: raising the pH factor, fertilizing the leaves and supplying the required trace elements.

Fungal attack

Fungi are parasites that attack weakened plants. They can only gain a hold on plants that have become stressed and weakened.

Mildew
Symptoms: White patches on buds and flowers. Spotty leaves, falling leaves and cessation of growth.
Causes: Too much humidity, extreme fluctuations in temperature.
Remedy: Move plants apart, remove dead and damaged parts (p. 22) and, if necessary, cut back a little. Spray regularly with a fungicide solution. The most vulnerable varieties are the *magellanica* species and their hybrids.

Rust
Symptoms: Discoloration of the leaves. A thin covering of something that looks like rust on new iron will appear on the undersides of the leaves. Later on, the leaves will fall, starting at the lowest branches.
Causes: Too much humidity, low temperatures, plants that have been

placed too close together.
Remedy: Remove affected leaves. Spray with a reputable fungicide every four days; later on, once a week.

Grey mould
Symptoms: Grey mould patches, especially on damaged parts of plants. Withering shoots.
Causes: Too much humidity, together with fluctuations in temperature in groups of plants that are

Pests
Left: Aphids.
Right: Californian thrips.

growing too close together and are being overfed. Not enough fresh air around the plants.
Remedy: Remove affected parts of the plants. Water in carefully controlled doses. Stop feeding or give plants a fertilizer containing extra potassium, which helps to strengthen plant tissues. Spray with a suitable fungicide. Provide plenty of fresh air.

Physiological disorders
These are caused by rhizoctonia, mainly in young plants.
Symptoms: The plant looks limp, even though the root stock is sufficiently moist, along with falling leaves and rotting of the lower stem and root system.
Causes: Too much fertilizing, waterlogging, soil that is too cold or soil that is packed too tight.
Remedy: Not really possible. Throw away affected plants but do *not* put them on your compost heap.

Preventive measures: Sterilize propagation containers and the pots used for young plants, for example, by immersing them in water which has been heated to over 50°C (122°F) for about ten minutes.

Pythium: root rot
Symptoms: Plants are withering.
Cause: Fungal infection via soil.
Remedy: Make sure the plant is subject to more even temperatures and careful watering. Water with a specific fungicide solution as recommended by a local nursery.

Pests

The appearance of pests is normally dependent on certain types of

Pests
Left: Spider mites.
Right: White fly.

weather. High pressure and temperatures above 25°C (77°F) favour aphids and red spider mites. Warm, damp conditions are ideal for cyclamen mites. Very often pests will migrate from neighbouring plants or are introduced via new plants.

Vine weevil
The main pest is the larva of the vine weevil. The beetle itself can only be observed at dusk as, during the day, it hides underground. It is worth checking for these pests in nooks and crannies under stones, logs and mulching layers in the vicinity.

Symptoms of vine weevil infestation: Parts eaten out of the edges of fully developed leaves.

Symptoms of larvae infestation: Damage is not so obvious as the larvae live exclusively underground and feed on the plant roots. If you suspect their presence, preventive treatment is the only way to deal with them. Methods of biological control, using natural predators, are being researched at the time of writing.

Cause: Introduction via compost or from other plants.

Remedy: Control of these pests is a long and tedious process. Using a torch to catch them at dusk or early evening is quite a successful method. Illuminated traps, baited with a layer of a sticky substance to lure the pests to their doom, have yielded good results. Biological methods are still being tested. Preventive measures are sterilization of the soil or compost, or mixing in a pesticide in prescribed proportions (ask for advice at your garden centre or fuchsia society).

Caterpillars

Symptoms: Chewed areas and small holes in parts of the plant above ground. The appearance of many tiny green caterpillars or the grey-green to brown caterpillars (up to 1 cm or ⅓ in) of the owlet moth. Black excrement.

Causes: Certain plants in the vicinity on which the moth prefers to deposit its eggs (for example, willow herb or other members of the order Onagraceae).

Remedy: Remove the caterpillars at dusk. If there is a severe infestation of these pests, spray the plants with a pesticide recommended by your local garden centre, carefully following the manufacturer's instructions.

Only one year old and already a lovely plant – the hanging variety "Cascade".

Red spider mites

(Illustration, p. 29.)

Symptoms: Discoloured, greyish-green leaves. Sparse growth; the undersides of leaves show spider-web-like structures full of tiny creatures. Severe infestation will lead to withering of the tips of the shoots and falling leaves.

Causes: Too warm, dry air (high pressure spells over 25°C or 77°F), badly ventilated rooms.

Remedy: Spray the undersides of leaves with a suitable pesticide. In a greenhouse with temperatures above 12°C (54°F), predating mites may be employed (enquire about these at your local garden centre).

White fly

(Illustration, p. 29.)

Symptoms: Tiny white insects which fly up as soon as the plant is touched. Tiny white scales (larvae) on the undersides of leaves, sticky secretions (honeydew) which encourage the growth of blackish, sooty mould (*Apio sporium*).

Causes: Stagnant air, invasion from other plants, overfed plants (too much fertilizer).

Remedy: Hang up sticky traps (see biological control, p. 28). Spray the whole plant but especially the undersides of the leaves with commercially available pesticides. At temperatures of above 18°C (69°F), ichneumon flies can be used as predators. Another successful method is spraying with a concoction of tansy, which must be sprayed on the plant three days in a row and preferably six to seven times.

Cyclamen mites

Symptoms: Crippled or stunted shoot tips but without visible holes.

Causes: Warm, damp weather favours the spread of these pests.

Remedy: Spray with a suitable pesticide. Cut affected parts back to healthy growth.

Aphids

(Illustration, p. 29.)

Symptoms: Dense colonies of aphids, which appear in various colours on young shoots. Crippling of young shoots. Deposits of honeydew secretions.

Causes: Lack of natural predators, warm, dry weather, plant tissues that are too soft because of unbalanced feeding.

Remedy: Spray the plants twice daily with a strong jet of water. Spray affected plants with an appropriate insecticide. Employ natural predators, such as the larvae of ladybirds, lacewing flies or the predatory gall midges (ask your garden society or local fuchsia society about sources of these).

Thrips (especially Californian thrips)

(Illustration, p. 29.)

Symptoms: Visible damage and drops of excrement on leaves. The pest itself is less than 1 mm long and can only be seen properly against a white background.

Cause: The larvae are the main problem. They hide in nooks and crannies inside flowers and in half-open buds. The plant cannot produce fruit. In cases of severe damage, cut back vigorously.

Remedy: At the time of writing the use of natural predators is not anticipated. Spray in rotation, using various special insecticides, as recommended by your garden centre.

Protection of indoor plants

Here, you must create a suitable environment for your plants as a preventive measure. This includes:
● good ventilation;
● providing sufficient shade;
● a means of increasing or reducing humidity;
● a source of heat from below.

Helpful insects

Certain insects find pests literally good enough to eat. They are most successfully employed *in a greenhouse* or in other closed rooms in which the temperature can be controlled. As soon as they have gobbled up your "enemies", they will tend to disappear. You may find order forms for natural predator insects at garden centres and nurseries. You could also enquire at your local gardening club or fuchsia society.

In the garden the most important allies are the ground beetles (Carabidae), ladybirds and their larvae, earwigs, hover flies (Syrphidae) and their larvae, ichneumon flies, spiders, hedgehogs, birds and shrews. All of these creatures will require cover, nesting places and colonies of plants on which to feed and lay eggs etc. (mixed cultivated and wild bushes and flowers). Prerequisites for the encouragement of such useful creatures are mulching layers, piles of dead leaves, wood piles, heaps of stones and clumps of bushes or trees.

Herbal sprays

You will need:

900 g (2 lb) each of coarsely chopped (or 100 g/3½ oz dried) common horsetail (*Equisetum*) and tansy (*Tanacetum vulgare*). Soak the horsetail and the tansy separately in 5 litres (1 gal) of water for 24 hours. Next day, bring each brew to the boil and allow it to simmer for half an hour. After they have cooled, strain the liquids. For spraying purposes, use one part horsetail tail brew with five parts tansy brew and three parts water.

Warning: Use all the brew in one spraying session! Keep it out of the reach of children – tansy brew is toxic!

Propagating fuchsias

If you wish to have several specimens of an especially attractive variety, simply cut off a shoot tip. Fuchsia shoots will root quickly and easily. You may even obtain several plantlets from a longer lateral, each of which will develop into a new plant. Propagation using seeds is much more difficult and is practised almost exclusively by hybridizers and specialists.

Propagating methods

Fuchsias can be propagated in various ways:
● From seeds. This method is called generative propagation as the genes of different parents have been combined. Propagation using seedlings from cultured fuchsias will produce offspring that are unlike the parents. Only pure wild species will produce young plants of the same species and variety when crossed. For the amateur, therefore, only vegetative propagation is recommended.
● From cuttings (illustration, p. 33). This method is called vegetative propagation. The offspring are exact copies of the mother plant.
● Another vegetative propagation method is to train a long, thin, trailing lateral to root in the ground (layering). It is only possible to do this during the fuchsia's main growing period.
● Propagation through offshoots, called stolon, which, in some species and varieties, are shoots that have developed underground in humus-rich soil and can then be detached from the mother plant.
● Through grafting (see p. 26).

My tip: The simplest and most successful way is vegetative propagation from parts of the plant.

Propagating equipment

Fuchsias can be propagated in various kinds of soil or compost or in water.

Suitable soils and composts:
● ready-mixed propagating and bedding composts;
● your own soil/compost mix made of moistened moss peat and washed, coarse sand in a ratio of 2:1;
● Perlite;
● fine Hortag;
● sand.

Other accessories:
● Protection against evaporation (see illustration). For single pots, a glass jar turned upside down or a transparent polythene bag with a few holes in it may be sufficient. Polythene sheeting "tents" can be built over beds or boxes, or light-permeable covers of other kinds may be used.
● Floor heating or a heatable propagation bed (this is especially important on cold window ledges).
● Rooting powder.
● Containers: clay or plastic pots with a diameter of less than 7 cm (3 in), peat pots, or trays with several compartments.

My tip: When rooting in water, the water must be kept at a consistently low level to prevent the plantlet from rotting. Use a flat container.

Propagating using cuttings

The most important prerequisite for propagation from cuttings is the choice of a healthy and vigorous mother plant.

Soft cuttings (illustration, p. 33) should preferably be taken from a plant with budless shoots. Using a sharp knife, cut off a shoot tip bearing two sets of leaves plus one that is just forming, immediately underneath the axil. Halve any particularly large leaves, in order to reduce the area of leaf surface that will lose water through evaporation. Try to avoid touching the cut edge. Dip the end of the stem into rooting powder and poke it into prepared compost or another medium, as described above.

Protection against evaporation
Left: Place a jar over the plant and press the rim lightly into the soil. Right: Use two crossed wires to make a dome and cover it with a plastic bag with a few holes in it.

Types of cuttings

Left: Cutting off a soft shoot tip, which will root very quickly.
Centre: Internode cutting with dormant buds in the leaf axils.
Right: Broken-off shoot with a trailing piece of bark, which is sure to form roots.

Lightly press down the soil and water it with a fine spray. Cover to prevent evaporation (see p. 32). **Woody shoots** should be finger-length, slightly woody laterals from the mother plant, which are removed by breaking them off downwards. Cut off the lowest set of leaves with their stalks and trim off any long strips of bark. Dip in rooting powder and poke into soil no deeper than 2.5-3 cm (½-1 in). Water.and cover (p. 32).

My tip: Hygiene is very important during the process of propagation from cuttings. Do not touch cut surfaces with your hands and avoid crushing or bruising the leaves as this can lead to decay. In order to prevent fungal infection, the cuttings can be given an initial watering with a fungicide.

Caring for cuttings

Their position should be bright, but not sunny.
Soil temperature should be a constant 18-20°C (64-68°F).
The air temperature should be kept within a range of 14-20°C (57-68°F), as long as the soil temperature is kept even. Stable, scarcely fluctuating temperatures are ideal.
Humidity should be kept high until the tenth day by using protection against evaporation (illustration, p. 32). Only then can the hood, polythene cover or jar be taken off occasionally for airing. After another four days, remove it completely. **Care** of the cuttings consists of checking them daily. Regularly remove any decayed parts and add extra water if the propagation medium has dried out.

Pricking out and potting on

Under ideal conditions, a soft cutting will root within 10 to 12 days and a woody cutting will root within three weeks. After a further 14 days, it is time to prick out the cuttings by transplanting them into separate 8-cm (3 in) pots. Good transplanting compost can be obtained from garden centres and nurseries. Keep the transplanted young plants sparingly moist and water them in the mornings only. As soon as the young fuchsias have grown to the point where the leaves touch each other, space the pots further apart. After about three weeks, you may fertilize them for the first time with a commercial fertilizer but do not exceed the recommended dose! In the spring and summer you may fertilize the leaves also. Spray a solution of 1-1.5 ml of fertilizer per litre (2 pt) of water onto the leaves, every two to three days – but never in the sun!

Repotting

When the roots of the young plants have spread right through the pot, the plant will have to be repotted! Now move it to a pot with a diameter of 10-12 cm (4-5 in). Use a standard potting compost and set the young plantlet in the earth no deeper than the stem stood in the previous pot.

Propagation using soft cuttings
Cut off a shoot tip (three sets of leaves without flowers). Dip the end of the stem in rooting powder, make a hole in the soil and poke the cutting in carefully so that the stem is not bent. (Pot 7 cm or 3 in.) Water sparingly and provide evaporation protection for the cutting (illustration, p. 32).

Propagation by layering

This method makes use of flexible laterals which are carefully trained down to touch the soil and then anchored there with a clip and covered with peat. Keep this peat cushion moist. After six to eight weeks, the rooted tip of the lateral can be separated from the mother plant.

Propagation by underground shoots

These shoots (stolons) appear all round the mother plant and will already have roots and leaves. All you have to do is separate them. If the mother plant is old and no longer at its best, dig it up and remove it, leaving the young plants to develop in ideal conditions.

Overwintering without problems

When night frosts are forecast, it is high time to move your fuchsias to their winter quarters. Before you do this, make a few essential preparations so that the plants will stay healthy and embark on maximum growth at the beginning of their next growing season. If you have never tried overwintering fuchsias before, you will be surprised at how easy it is.

Winter feeding

The finer the woody parts are, the better the plant will survive the dark time of year. From late summer onwards, only use fertilizers with a phosphorus-potassium base, as recommended by your garden centre or nursery. Follow the manufacturer's instructions carefully when judging the correct amount to use.

Watering

From early autumn on, you may reduce the amount of water given. As the nights become cooler and dew starts falling again, the plant will absorb quite a large amount of moisture through its above-ground parts. The root stock, too, will not dry out as fast as in the summer. On hot, sunny days during the first and second months of autumn, in the type of conditions that are especially common in the wine-growing areas of Europe, caution is called for as the root stock must not be allowed to dry out at any cost.

Moving bedding fuchsias

Frost often appears earlier than expected. Remember to dig out budding fuchsias in good time. Once they are in pots, they may be left outside until shortly before the first frosts are due.

Method:
● Dig up the root stock with extra earth so that it is larger than the container or pot.
● Reduce the root volume a little by hand and stand it loosely in the pot.
● Fill in extra earth around the sides of the pot and make sure it is well and evenly distributed.
● Do not press the earth down too firmly so that it does not become compacted.
● Water lightly and place the pot in a sheltered position until it is time to take it inside.

Pruning for overwintering

This is not absolutely essential, but is recommended if:
● the tips of the shoots are still too soft and delicate;
● the overwintering area is limited;

"Satellite"

"Pink Marshmallow"

"Marcus Graham"

"American Prelude"

"Blue Satin"

"Centrepiece"

- the plants are too wide (laterals too long);
- the shoots have lots of flowers, buds and fruit, which will only drop later on and have to be swept up (because of the danger of grey mould).

Simply cut off the last third of each branch. If you have not much room for your plants, except for dark, damp winter quarters, you should use the preventive measure of spraying them beforehand with a fungicide so that no fungal spores can settle in the fresh cuts.

My tip: Many experienced fuchsia lovers cut off every leaf, leaving only part of the stalk. This is especially advisable if the plant has been infested.

Positions for overwintering

The ideal place for fuchsias to over-winter will be cool, humid and bright. As the fuchsia is deciduous, it can also overwinter in a dark room. One proviso, however, is that the plant should be fairly woody.

Young plants without woody parts are best placed on a windowsill for overwintering, at a temperature between 10 and 15°C (50-59°F).
NB: If you do not have a cool posi-tion for overwintering, you must provide extra light, otherwise the plants will become rank and weak (p. 28).

Overwintering above ground or in earth pits
This kind of overwintering site is ideal for those people who have many fuchsias and also own a garden.

Above ground the fuchsias can be stored for overwintering by standing the plants close together, sprinkling earth or dead leaves over them, then, to provide a frost-proof top layer, placing some 30 cm (12 in) of beech leaves over that and covering them with branches to anchor the leaves. *An earth pit* is another overwintering device (illustration, p. 38). Dig a pit that is at least 80 cm (30 in) deep. Choose a place that will not be flooded every time it rains and where the water level is not close to the surface. Plants are placed on their sides in the pit. The spaces between the plants should be filled with dry peat, dry beech leaves, crumpled up newspapers or polystyrene flakes. If you have any reason to suspect that mice might be a problem, first line the pit with narrow-gauge chicken wire. Finally, cover it all over with planks. Place another 30-cm (12 in) layer of dead leaves on top and anchor this with branches.
NB: Both methods provide dark winter quarters which are only suitable for very woody plants. They can be left here until the middle of spring.

Overwintering in composting pits

These are ideal if they are dug deep enough (at least 60 cm or 2 ft deep) and the walls are clad with an additional, insulating layer of polystyrene sheeting. Fill the pit with small or large fuchsia plants and cover it with a double-glazed frame and reed matting. On frost-free days, take the cover off and air the pit.

Fuchsias in combination with other plants
A compact bush fuchsia called "Beacon Rosa" (top), followed (centre) by the pure red cultivar "Kwintett" and (below) a spreading cushion of Felicia ammelloides.

After the spring pruning, the fuchsias may be left in the pit until they develop shoots and buds.

Subterranean greenhouses

These are rather rare nowadays. They are greenhouses that sit below ground level up to the edge of the roof and require hardly any heating. When temperatures drop very low, just cover them completely with straw mats. In this type of greenhouse, you can allow the plants to begin shooting again in the early spring.

Light shafts

These can be used if you have cellar or basement windows below ground level with a horizontal grating set into the ground. Simply cover the grating with polythene sheeting or glass. In cold weather, open the cellar window (inwards) in order to allow warmer air to rise from inside the cellar.

Outside cellar steps

This may be a good solution if you do not use the steps much during the winter months. Cover the steps with glass or polythene sheeting and use them to store plants. Again, you may wish to open the cellar door occasionally to allow warmth from the cellar to rise up the steps and equalize the temperature.

Dark cellars

Cellars provide ideal winter quarters for fuchsias but the temperature should never rise above 8°C (46°F). If it does, it will become necessary to provide additional light as well.

Attics and lofts

Attics that are safe from frost, with large, double-glazed windows for airing, provide ideal conditions for overwintering and are useful for encouraging the growth of new shoots on your fuchsia plants in the spring.

Indoors

Indoor rooms are only useful if they are heated sparingly. Place the plants directly in a window and never allow the temperature to rise above 12°C (54°F).

Conservatories

Here, plants will keep their leaves and winter-flowering plants will flourish (see p. 58). Check that the foundations are frost-proof as, during long, cold periods, the cold may seep upwards through the foundations into the floor and damage the plants. Temperatures may fluctuate slightly between above freezing to room temperature.

Greenhouses

Again, check that the foundations are frost-proof. Until early spring, overwintering temperatures of between 0-6°C (32-43°F) will be adequate. If young plants are also overwintering, the temperature must be raised to above 12°C (54°F).

My tip: Check the temperature around all overwintering plants every week and make sure the roots are sufficiently moist (except in overwintering pits). Use a special mini-max temperature thermometer which can be purchased at garden centres etc. If necessary, install a frost guard, which will automatically switch on the heating system as soon as the temperature has dropped beneath the set minimum.

Using electric lighting

At temperatures of below 6°C (43°F), fuchsias are dormant. If kept at this temperature, they can overwinter in a dark cellar. If the temperature rises to above 8°C (46°F), and if natural daylight is not available, they will have to be lit artificially.

Clay heating tubes will prevent the fuchsias from forming pale shoots without chlorophyll in a warm environment, which would tend to sap their strength. These tubes are suspended about 60 cm (2 ft) above the plants. You will require approximately one double tube per metre (3 ft) of plant spread (obtainable from garden centres or electrical suppliers).
Growth lamps will be required if you are intending to grow young plants in overwintering quarters. One growth lamp has an ouput of about 2500 lux. The young fuchsias will need this lighting for about 11 hours per day. Later, if they are to be forced during the flowering period, about two hours' extra lighting will be needed. It will make no difference whether you use the lights during the day or night.

Care of dormant plants

Although fuchsias are generally going through a dormant phase in their winter quarters, you will still need to keep an eye on them and give them some care.

Overwintering in an earth pit
Dig a pit 80 cm (30 in) deep, line the sides with narrow-gauge chicken wire and cover with wooden planks that overlap at the edge of the pit. Cover the top with a 30 cm (12 in) layer of dead leaves.

Watering is still important during the winter. Even a dormant, older, woody fuchsia may dry out completely and wither in its winter quarters. For this reason, checking the moisture of the root stock at intervals of one to three weeks (depending on temperatures and lighting) is very important. The warmer and brighter the conditions, the more often you will have to water the plants. If the water runs off the root stock, it is too dry and will have to be immersed in water. Too much water, on the other hand, can result in woodier plants dying. Always make sure the drainage holes are clear, that the container is well drained and is not standing directly on the ground.
Airing will prevent infestation by pests and fungi. On days when outside temperatures are above freezing, open the windows and doors.
Protecting your plants may become necessary if they are kept in unsuitable places. Watch out for grey mould and rust (p. 29). If your plants become diseased or infested with pests, first try to improve the environmental conditions. If that does not work, use an appropriate insecticide or fungicide (p. 31).

Cutting back in the spring

When to cut back will depend largely on the kind of growth conditions you can offer your plants after they have developed young shoots. Higher temperatures and brightly lit rooms which are well ventilated, are vital for the development of healthy shoots. The later you leave the pruning back, the later the flowers will form. First remove weak shoots and ones that cross so that they will not rub against each other.

The fuchsia year
In the second month of the winter

Bush fuchsias in spring
Spring pruning should remove weak or crossed shoots completely. Cut back year-old shoots to the first to third axils, depending on the thickness of the shoot. Consider the total shape of the plant while doing this.

Removing the soft shoot tips will encourage the development of four times as many flowers and a compact shaped head.

season, you may begin to prune all fuchsias that are overwintering in conservatories or greenhouses at room temperatures.
The new shoots will supply cuttings for growing on into new young plants.
From the last month of winter onwards, cut back plants that have been standing in a cold greenhouse, in a conservatory, on a veranda covered over with glass or on covered cellar steps.
From the second month of spring onwards, plants that have been standing in darker positions, such as stairwells, a cellar or in a dimly lit attic, are due for pruning.
Fuchsias that are destined for a position on a sheltered balcony may be pruned right *up until the beginning of the last month of spring.*

How to prune

Pruning will depend greatly on the shape of the fuchsia.

For bushes and pyramids (illustration, p. 38), take the year-old shoots – these are the tips of laterals which have not forked and from which the tips have already been removed in the autumn (p. 38) – and, depending on their thickness, cut them back to one or two axils. Always take into consideration the shape in which the plant is growing and loosen any ties that seem too tight and which might constrict the stem.

My tip: Do not throw away a fuchsia bush, even if its head has suffered frost damage right down to the stem! Cut it back to the healthy woody parts and build up a new head out of the young shoots (see p. 25).

When pruning **hanging plants**, look for characteristics that are typical of that variety. These plants should be cut in such a way that they will flower as early as possible. If hanging fuchsias are cut back too much, that is, back to one to three axils per branch, you will end up with young shoots that are too sturdy. Right from the beginning, they will tend not to form the shape of a hanging plant. The increasing weight of buds and flowers will pull the laterals downwards in such a

way that the centre of the hanging plant remains relatively flat. For this reason, when using varieties with long branches, cut the main branches back to only two-thirds of their length, but try to retain the laterals and cut them back to one or two axils. Make sure that you cut the shoots back a bit more in the centre of the plant so that you will obtain a bushier centre. This method is used particularly with varieties like "Gesäuseperle", "Marinka", "Lena", "Achievement", "Lolita" and "Mantilla".

Varieties that branch out vigorously and quickly attain the desired hanging shape, can be cut back even more rigorously (examples: "La Campanella", "Harry Gray" and "Multa").

Older, bushy plants should be left with longer lower laterals if they are thick and strong. Cut back only the tips by about a third. The laterals should be cut back to one to four axils.

Damaged plants should be cut right back to the healthy, woody parts. The shoots that will appear later on, which are thick but not very numerous, should have their soft tips cut out (illustration, p. 19).

Pruning back bush fuchsias
For bushes with a single main stem, this will determine the desired height. The laterals are cut back to one or two axils.

Care after cutting back

As well as increasing light and warmth, spring pruning will stimulate the fuchsia to new growth. During this phase, plants have to be watched carefully!

Watering after dormancy

After the first pruning, water your plants once thoroughly to activate new shoots. After that, just keep the soil moist so that newly forming rootlets can absorb sufficient oxygen. Too much moisture will lead to decaying roots. This will become obvious when new shoots appear to "withdraw" again.

First aid: Immediately cut the roots back to healthy tissue (this will be light-coloured instead of brownish or decayed) and replant the plant in a smaller clay pot, which will make it easier for the roots to breathe. Water once, sparingly.

Feeding after dormancy

In general, this should not be done until the new shoots show properly developed leaves.
Suitable fertilizers are:
● liquid fertilizers, which are applied to the moist root stock once a week (2-3 ml per litre or 2 pt of water);

Trimming the root stock

Roots reaching right to the edge of the pot should be cut back all round by about a third to a quarter of the roots. Put the root stock back in the same (scrubbed) pot at the same depth as before but with new soil.

● long-lasting fertilizers, which are sprinkled once only on to the root stock (3 g per litre or 2 pt of earth);
● organic multi-fertilizer (for the correct dosage, follow the manufacturer's instructions).

Repotting

Only repot when the soil has been used up or the root stock is completely matted. In the case of young fuchsias, the new container should be at least 2 cm (⅘ in) larger than the old one. Large, older specimens, in containers of more than 45 cm (18 in) diameter, need repotting only once every few years. They should be put back in the same container (scrub it well first!) after the root stock has been trimmed back (illustration, p. 39). At this time you should also check tied-back parts and support sticks.

Method:

● With varieties that root reluctantly, just carefully shake off some of the soil.
● With vigorously rooting fuchsias, remove the lower quarter of the root stock and break off the upper edge.
● In the case of older, matted root stocks, remove a third, all the way round, with a sharp knife.
NB: Repotted fuchsias will not require feeding for about four or five weeks. The new soil should supply enough nutrients until then.

Gentle pruning

This is recommended for all shaped, solitary plants when the shoot is one fingerlength long. Only the tip is removed, so that three to five axils remain (illustration, p. 19). This will stimulate the growth of many new shoots, a compact shape and a profusion of flowers.

The right position

The place where a fuchsia is kept should, initially, have a temperature

The fuchsia "Small Pipes" – a gem among the newer cultivars.

of 16-20° C (61-68° F) and be airy and bright until the shoots appear. After that, drop the temperature to 10-14° C (50-57° F). From the second month of spring onwards, the fuchsias may be placed in glass or polythene-covered greenhouses.

Fuchsias in the greenhouse

Owning a small greenhouse is the ambition of most plant lovers. Here, young fuchsia plants can be grown to maturity, bush fuchsias grown to the right shape and all plants left to overwinter and shoot naturally. Just how extensively you use your greenhouse and how you decide to grow your fuchsias will depend on the temperatures that you create and on several other important factors.
The greenhouse should:
● be as close to the house as pos-

sible, because of supply lines (electricity, water, heating);
● have well-insulated foundations;
● have windows and ventilation facilities, as well as two doors situated opposite each other, so that there is always fresh air and, in summer, fresh air can circulate;
● have a ventilator;
● be equipped with a thermometer, a hygrometer (to measure humidity) and a frost guard.
With a minimum of heating, an **unheated greenhouse** can be kept warm in winter at a temperature of 3-5° C (37-41° F). At night, a thermostat will ensure that the temperature remains constant. This cold house is ideal for overwintering fuchsias and other plants in containers.
At the beginning of the last month of winter, when the days are becoming noticeably longer and

Protecting plants in the greenhouse

Hygiene and preventive measures are essential in a small greenhouse. Watch out for botrytis, rust, aphids, white fly and red spider mites as soon as the plants start growing. Ensure that growing conditions are optimal, which means:
● constant temperatures!
● constant humidity!
● good ventilation!
Do not stand the plants too close together and only water before noon, so that the foliage has time to dry off during the day.

Early flowering without a greenhouse

If you keep your fuchsias in the following places, you can count on early flowering:
● in a polythene tunnel;
● in a lean-to greenhouse on a patio or balcony. This is easy to make yourself by building a frame out of battens and stretching strong, transparent polythene sheeting over it. Lean-to greenhouses are also obtainable from garden centres etc.;
● in a composting pit;
● on outside cellar steps covered over with glass or polythene sheets;
● in attics with large windows.
Fuchsias that are placed here will start flowering earlier than those placed in a sheltered position outside.

From the Colombian rainforest – Fuchsia hartwegii.

lighter, your fuchsias will start to produce shoots. Now, you can start rooting cuttings in small, heatable propagation beds. A greenhouse is also a suitable place to start fuchsias shooting in the early spring, especially if they have overwintered in a dark place. It is also ideal for housing plants that have spent the winter under artificial light.
A heated greenhouse will provide even more scope. During the winter months it should be kept at a daytime temperature of 12-16° C (54-61° F), and, at night, at 6-10° C (43-50° F). Many of the plants placed here in the autumn will push out lots of healthy, new shoots and produce flowers. Good flowering results may be obtained with winter-flowering species, such as *Fuchsia speciosa, Fuchsia arborescens*, and the cultivars "First Success" or "Miep Aalhuizen" at temperatures above 6° C (43° F).

In a temperature-controlled greenhouse the pruning of other fuchsia varieties can begin as early as the second month of the winter season. In the early spring, cut out soft shoot tips, and, during the second month of spring, repeat pruning, if necessary.

My tip: The shoot tips you have cut out make ideal material for cuttings (p. 32). In a bright greenhouse you may also start fertilizing earlier. As soon as new shoots appear, begin fertilizing once a week with a liquid concentrated fertilizer (2 ml per litre or 2 pt of water). From this point on, fertilizing the leaves with 1-1.5 ml per litre (2 pt) of water is also possible. If the plant has been repotted, do not feed it until the roots have spread out into the pot. As a rule, this will take four to five weeks.

A selection of exquisite fuchsias

You will soon discover that there is an astonishing array of lovely fuchsia species and varieties. A selection of the myriad flower colours and shapes available will be found in the colour photographs on the following pages. Here, no matter what your preferences are, you will find inspiration and ideas for turning your garden, patio, terrace or balcony into an enchanted garden.

Key terms

The first part of the name is always the name of a fuchsia. Quotation marks indicate that it is a hybridized variety or cultivar.

Raiser or hybridizer: This will give you the name of the person who first raised the fuchsia, the year it was created and its country of origin.

Origin: In the case of naturally occurring fuchsias, this will give the name of the part of the world it comes from.

Flower: A description of the shape of the flower (single, semi-double, or double, see illustration, p. 9). The secondary descriptions give the colours and shapes of the tube, sepals, corolla, stamens and stigma (illustration, p. 9). The colour descriptions given are the ideal, typical ones for the particular variety but too much sunlight, for example, can alter the colour of a flower.

Leaves: These are generally subordinate to the flowers but are surprisingly diverse.

An easy-to-care-for, permanent-flowering cultivar
This fuchsia, "Winston Churchill", bred in 1942 in the USA, quickly became a firm favourite.

Growth: A distinction is made between upright, semi-hanging and hanging types. The words "compact growth" are used to describe plants that branch out well at short intervals.

Use: This describes the conditions for which the particular variety is especially suited.

● A "solitary plant" is usually a lone-standing fuchsia with an especially attractive total appearance. It may be planted in a container or in a bed.

● Fuchsias recommended as bedding plants will do especially well in such a position. They will be robust, grow upright and bushy and be full of flowers. If you want to enjoy them again the following year, you will have to dig them up in the autumn and allow them to overwinter in a frost-free position (see p. 34).

● "Hardy" varieties should also be planted in beds and should be treated like any other garden shrubs for overwintering (p. 14). "Semi-hardy" means that this fuchsia can only be left to overwinter outside in a sheltered position with some kind of protection (such as heaping dead leaves or peat over it).

Varieties/cultivars and species

The page numbers indicate where you will find exact descriptions and colour photographs of the particular varieties/cultivars or species.

"Alison Ewart" 57
"Annabel" 46
"Cecile" 47
"Cliantha" 50
"Countess of Aberdeen" 53
"Daisy Bell" 52
"Dark Eyes" 46
"Delice" 44
"Elfriede Ott" 49
"Forget-Me-Not" 53
Fuchsia arborescens 58
Fuchsia boliviana var. luxurians
"Alba" 58
Fuchsia denticulata 58
Fuchsia magellanica var.
macrostemma (syn. var. gracilis)
59
Fuchsia paniculata 58
Fuchsia speciosa 58
"General Monk" 44
"Gesäuseperle" 48
"Göttingen" 49
"Happy" 56
"Hawkshead" 56
"Hummeltje" 56
"Joy Patmore" 45
"La Campanella" 56
"Leonhart von Fuchs" 54
"Little Beauty" 44
"Lolita" 52
"Loni Jane" 50
"Mrs Lovell Swisher" 52
"Nettala" 54
"Paula Jane" 44
"Pennine" 46
"Pink Quartette" 51
"Ron Ewart" 44
"Son of Thumb" 56
"Southgate" 46
"Tinker Bell" 52
"Vielliebchen" 57
"Vobeglo" 55
"Wilson's Pearls" 44

A colourful kaleidoscope of more recent fuchsia cultivars.

1 "Ron Ewart"

Raiser: Roe, 1981, Britain
Flower: single
Tube: white, short, thick
Sepals: white, short and wide, standing upright
Corolla: dark pink, short
Leaves: medium green
Growth: upright
Use: bedding and solitary plants

2 "General Monk"

Raiser: unknown
Flower: double
Tube: cherry red
Sepals: cherry red
Corolla: brilliant blue, whitish base, slightly pink-veined
Leaves: dark green
Growth: upright, com-pact, branches well
Use: ideal bedding plant. Also suitable for edging along with other varieties and in combination with other plants

3 "Delice"

Raiser: De Graaff, 1984, Netherlands
Flower: single
Tube: light pink
Sepals: Light pink, semi-upright
Corolla: dark pink
Leaves: medium sized
Growth: hanging
Use: for hanging baskets and espaliers

4 "Little Beauty"

Raiser: unknown
Flower: single
Tube: light red
Sepals: light red
Corolla: lavender blue, short
Leaves: medium green, small, narrow
Growth: upright
Use: versatile (also for bonsai), hardy (flower bed)

5 "Wilson's Pearls"

Raiser: Wilson, 1967, Britain
Flower: single
Tube: red
Sepals: red, narrow, turned up
Corolla: white with pink veins
Leaves: light green, nar-row, pointed
Growth: hanging
Use: excellent for hang-ing baskets and solitary plants

6 "Paula Jane"

Raiser: Tite, 1975, Britain
Flower: semi-double
Tube: pink
Sepals: carmine pink, standing upright
Corolla: dark ruby red
Leaves: upright, com-pact, well branched
Use: a robust bedding plant

"Joy Patmore"

Raiser: Turner, 1961, USA

Flower: single, especially beautiful bell shape

Tube: short, thick, white

Sepals: waxy white, wide at the base but tapering to a point, upright

Corolla: brilliant carmine red, white at base

Stamen: pink

Stigma: white

Leaves: dark green, broad

Growth: upright and bushy but a little spindly. This everlasting flowering variety captivates at a distance with its especially clear, striking colours. Even at the budding stage, the masses of white buds draw one's gaze

Use: Very often to be found as a bedding plant or solitary plant

My tip: This attractive variety grows with a profusion of leaves, but will adapt easily to a bush shape or a pyramid shape. How to achieve these shapes is explained on p. 25. Very suitable for the beginner!

A favourite for patios and balconies – this variety displays striking, cheerful colours.

An infinite variety of shape and colour characterizes these cultivars.

1 "Dark Eyes"

Raiser: Erickson, 1958, USA
Flower: double
Tube: carmine red
Sepals: carmine red
Corolla: clear blue, with a pink base. Edges of petals are rolled in slightly, achieving an especially attractive effect. Regular shape
Stamen: pink
Stigma: pink
Leaves: dark green, reddish veins, slightly convex
Growth: hanging
Use: Classic hanging type, becoming ever more popular. Very suitable for a semi-shady position

2 "Annabel"

Raiser: Ryle, 1977, Britain
Flower: double
Tube: white and pink stripes, long
Sepals: whitish-pink, broad, upright
Corolla: white with delicate pink veins
Stamen: light pink
Stigma: light pink
Leaves: light green, dentate edges, slightly concave
Growth: upright and slightly hanging
Use: bedding plant or in containers
NB: In semi-sunny to sunny positions, the pink colouring will intensify.

3 "Southgate"

Raiser: Walker & Jones, 1951, USA
Flower: double
Tube: pale pink
Sepals: pale pink with greenish tips, standing upright
Corolla: light pink, slightly veined
Stamen: light pink
Stigma: white
Leaves: medium sized, medium green, broad, serrated, reddish stalks
Growth: hanging
Use: ideal for large hanging baskets and as a solitary plant. Weather-hardy, large flowers, very popular, universal variety

4 "Pennine"

Raiser: Mitchinson, 1981, Britain
Flower: single
Tube: red with dark lines
Sepals: white, reddish base
Corolla: violet blue
Stamen: pink
Stigma: whitish
Leaves: dark green, medium sized, serrated
Growth: upright, bushy
Use: robust, white-violet variety with excellent characteristics as a bedding, container or solitary plant. Vigorous growth

"Cecile"

Raiser: Whitfield, 1981, USA
Flower: double
Tube: pink, short
Sepals: reddish pink, upright
Corolla: lavender blue with pink base. Each petal is wavy
Stamen: pink
Stigma: light pink
Leaves: medium green
Growth: hanging, well branched
Use: most suited to large hanging baskets and containers. Supple growth and rich profusion of flowers (the flowers are medium sized and they appear especially attractive as the petals are wavy)

My tip: For a hanging basket of 25-30 cm (10-12 in) in diameter, allow for five fuchsia plants. As a solitary plant, it is capable of filling a container with a diameter of 30 cm (12 in) by its second year. The plant will then be approximately 80 cm (18 in) tall.

"Cecile" – a gardener's dream, whether in a hanging basket or as a bush.

A typical triphylla hybrid – "Göttingen".

Triphylla hybrids always have long tubes.

"Gesäuseperle"

Raiser: Nutzinger, 1946, Austria
Flower: single
Tube: creamy white
Sepals: white
Corolla: red
Stamen: pinkish-white
Stigma: white
Leaves: medium green, large surface, serrated
Growth: young laterals are slightly upright, laterals in full flower tend to hang down markedly
Use: Suitable for hanging baskets, flower boxes and containers. Will cope with semi-sunny position
NB: Looks very similar to the old variety, "Amelie Aubin" (1884).

1 "Göttingen"

Raiser: Bonstedt, 1904, Germany
Flower: single, flowers in a raceme
Tube: brilliant orange, with a swelling
Sepals: orange
Corolla: cinnobar red
Leaves: large surface, dark, reddish underside
Growth: upright, bushy, medium tall
Use: as a bedding plant or in containers. A commanding appearance with a profusion of flowers in glorious colours against a background of much darker foliage. The individual flower has an interesting shape

2 "Elfriede Ott"

Raiser: Nutzinger, 1977, Austria
Flower: single
Tube: old rose, long, thick
Sepals: salmon pink
Corolla: dark pink
Stamen: salmon pink
Stigma: salmon pink
Leaves: light green, red central vein, slightly hairy
Growth: hanging
Use: popular as a hanging or bedding variety

My tip: This fuchsia is a *triphylla* hybrid, just like the variety "Göttingen", and should be treated in the same way. *Triphylla* hybrids can cope better with sun-

light than other varieties. They should overwinter in bright surroundings and at a higher than average temperature (10°C / 50°F or above) than other fuchsias. In a room or heated conservatory, they will flower in winter if they are kept at a temperature of about 15°C (59°F). Even when in hanging baskets and flower boxes, this variety loves a warmer, more sheltered position. Encouraging the formation of shoots may be a little difficult, as this variety produces flowerbuds throughout most seasons of the year. The buds on a cutting should be pinched out sideways, very carefully

"Cliantha" – introducing a new cultivar.

The frothy double flower of "Loni Jane".

1 "Cliantha"

Raiser: Strümper, 1985, Germany
Flower: double
Tube: pinkish-red
Sepals: pinkish-red with green tips
Corolla: light violet with a darker base
Stamen: pink, violet
Stigma: light pink
Leaves: medium sized, medium green
Growth: upright, bushy, slightly hanging
Use: bedding and container plant. Well suited for use in large hanging baskets

My tip: Hang your hanging basket on a rope and pulley, then just lower the basket for watering. This method is also useful for deadheading and trimming.

2 "Loni Jane"

Raiser: unknown
Flower: double
Tube: pale pink
Sepals: white with a pale pink blush
Corolla: white with a pale pink blush
Stamen: reddish-pink
Stigma: reddish-pink
Leaves: large, light green
Growth: hanging
Use: for large hanging baskets

My tip: Use at least five plants for a hanging basket with a diameter of 25-30 cm (10-12 in).

NB: This unusual variety draws the onlooker's gaze like a magnet when the first flowers open up. It is safe to say that it is one of those varieties that can turn even an impartial observer into a collector and lover of fuchsias. In order to obtain a bushy appearance, it must be pruned back at least twice, as the internodes are very long. There is an amazing resemblance to the varieties "Snowy Summit", "Pink Marshmallow", and "Icicle".

"Pink Quartette"

Raiser: Walker & Jones, 1949, USA
Flower: semi-double
Tube: pink
Sepals: dark pink, broad, upright
Corolla: whitish-pink, slightly veined
Stamen: pink
Stigma: pink
Leaves: dark green, large surface
Growth: upright, stiff, branches out only reluctantly
Use: as a container plant or a shaped, solitary plant. Robust variety
Special feature: The large, profusely distributed flowers form their petals into four exactly equal, separate corolla. The set of stamens and the stigma, however, appear only once. The flower is especially attractive and lasts a very long time

My tip: Give this variety plenty of room. By cutting out additional short tips, the slightly spindly, stiff growth can be trained a little better and will make the plant produce about four times as many flowers. Use only large containers and plant smaller plants underneath.

"Pink Quartette" – each flower produces four sets of petals.

A small selection from the profusion of American fuchsia cultivars.

1 "Mrs Lovell Swisher"

Raiser: Evans & Reeves, 1942, USA
Flower: single
Tube: pink
Sepals: whitish, pink undersides, greenish tips
Corolla: dark pink with a reddish tinge, lighter at the base, small
Stamen: dark pink
Stigma: pink
Leaves: medium green, pale
Growth: upright, spindly
Use: suitable as a bedding and container plant. Especially beautiful as a shaped solitary plant. Bush shaped plants will form a densely foliated head

2 "Daisy Bell"

Raiser: unknown
Flower: single
Tube: whitish, orange blush
Sepals: light orange with whitish-green tips
Corolla: salmon pink with green tips
Stamen: pale pink
Stigma: cream
Leaves: light green, copper-red tinge
Growth: hanging
Use: flower boxes and hanging baskets in a semi-sunny to sunny position. Vigorous growth

My tip: Like all fuchsias with coloured foliage, it should not be given too much water.

3 "Tinker Bell"

Raiser: Hodges, 1955, USA
Flower: single
Tube: whitish-pink
Sepals: whitish-pink with red tips, dark pink undersides
Corolla: light pink, lightly veined
Stamen: dark pink
Stigma: white
Leaves: medium green, narrow, long
Growth: hanging
Use: elegant, vigorously growing, long-flowering plant for hanging baskets

4 "Lolita"

Raiser: Tiret, 1963, USA
Flower: double
Tube: whitish-pink
Sepals: whitish-pink, green tips, dark pink underside
Corolla: violet blue with pink veins
Stamen: pink
Stigma: whitish-pink
Leaves: narrow, light green, pointed
Growth: hanging
Use: extravagant hanging basket variety. Not suitable for very shady positions

My tip: Start pinching out shoot tips early.

"Forget-Me-Not" – an old English variety.

An English fuchsia from the Victorian era.

1 "Forget-Me-Not"

Raiser: Banks, 1866, Britain
Flower: single
Tube: light pink
Sepals: light pink
Corolla: blue violet
Stamen: pink
Stigma: pink
Leaves: medium large, shiny, medium green
Growth: upright, spindly
Use: as a container plant or solitary plant
NB: This old variety, which bears many flowers, has retained its vitality well over the years and is an old, established gem among solitary plants.

Other older, small, profusely flowering varieties:

The following fuchsias bear single flowers and grow upright and bushy.

(Colours: sepals/corolla)
"Bon Accord", 1861, white/pinkish purple
"Chillerton Beauty", 1847, pink/blue violet
"Elysee", 1886, red/violet
"Graf Witte", 1899, red/purple
"Lustre", 1868, cream/salmon-pink
"Madame van der Strass", 1878, cherry red/white
"Rose of Castille", 1855, white/purple

2 "Countess of Aberdeen"

Raiser: Dobbie Forbes, 1888, Britain
Flower: single
Tube: white
Sepals: pale pink
Corolla: white, pink blush
Stamen: pale pink
Stigma: white
Leaves: small, concave, serrated, medium green
Growth: low, bushy
Use: as a pot, bedding, container and solitary plant
NB: Popular, old variety with a profusion of dainty flowers, especially suitable for keeping indoors.

Tips on care and propagation

Always keep your fuchsias in a shady position, otherwise the white flowers will discolour. This variety is especially susceptible to grey mould infestation (see p. 29). If the plant is affected, remove the diseased parts, water less, change to a fertilizer that contains more phosphorus and potassium and spray the plant with a fungicide. Use only soft shoot cuttings for propagation (illustration, p. 33). Cuttings from this variety will usually require more time than other fuchsias for root formation.

A record breaker – the fuchsia with the longest flowers.

Unusual flowers – petals on stalks.

1 "Leonhart von Fuchs"

Raiser: Strümper, 1985, Germany
Flower: single
Tube: orange red, extremely long
Sepals: orange with green tips, short
Corolla: orange red
Stamen: light orange
Stigma: light orange
Leaves: large, light green, reddish-brown shoot tips
Growth: hanging
Use: for hanging baskets. This is purely a collector's variety
NB: Of all known fuchsias at this time, "Leonhart von Fuchs" has the longest flowers (up to 18 cm or 7 in long).

How to identify a collector's variety:
Some varieties have especially fascinating features but may also have less favourable characteristics, which prevent them from becoming widely popular. Such a variety will especially appeal to lovers of unusually attractive flowers. Its disadvantages are usually that:
● it does not branch out well;
● there are few shoots;
● the cuttings do not root well;
● after the first rush of blooms, the plant loses its older leaves;
● its shoots break off easily.

2 "Nettala" ▲

Raiser: Francesca, 1973, USA
Flower: single
Tube: dark red, short and thick
Sepals: dark red, short
Corolla: violet red, petals with stalks
Stamen: white
Stigma: white
Leaves: medium sized, medium green
Growth: upright, bushy
Use: especially suited to shaping into a standard
NB: This speciality among fuchsia flower shapes cries out to be studied close-up and preferably displayed as a standard. The long-stalked petals are enhanced by the white filaments. A well-known variety for hanging baskets, with similar characteristics, but slightly smaller flowers, is the variety:

"Pussy Cat"

Raiser: Felix, 1978, Netherlands
Flower: single
Sepals: salmon pink
Corolla: orange pink
Growth: semi-hanging

"Vobeglo"

Raiser: De Groot, 1974, Netherlands
Flower: single
Tube: bright pink, short and thick
Sepals: bright pink
Corolla: violet purple with a lighter base
Stamen: pink
Stigma: pale pink
Leaves: medium green, small
Growth: upright, compact. The numerous shoots are very upright and have short internodes. Training a bush or standard will require much care. As the shoots break off very easily, the plant has to be well supported and the stem has to be tied to the support at close intervals
Use: especially as a pot plant but also as a bedding, tub, basin, or solitary plant. Very attractive, with upright flowers which remind one of azaleas in appearance. Give "Vobeglo" a semi-sunny position, well sheltered from the wind
NB: "Vobeglo" is one of the few varieties whose ancestors are known in detail. Its family tree is as follows:
Grandparents: *Fuchsia regia typica* and "Bon Accord".
Parents: "Pallas" and "Frau Henriette Ernst".

"Vobeglo" has a cheerful, sprightly appearance and its flowers are reminiscent of azalea blooms.

Some fuchsia flowers create an especially interesting effect with their long, prominent styles.

1 "La Campanella"

Raiser: Blackwell, 1968, Britain
Flower: semi-double
Tube: white
Sepals: white with a pink blush
Corolla: purple violet
Leaves: small, medium green,
Growth: hanging
Use: for large containers, tubs, and hanging baskets.

2 "Son of Thumb"

Raiser: Gubler, 1978, Britain
Flower: single
Tube: cherry red
Sepals: cherry red
Corolla: violet, small
Leaves: small, medium green
Growth: upright, compact
Use: in pots, beds, tubs, and containers

3 "Hawkshead"

Raiser: Travis, 1962, Britain
Flower: single, small flower
Tube: white
Sepals: white, slightly curved
Corolla: white, slightly curved
Stamen: white
Stigma: white
Leaves: dark green, narrow
Growth: upright, stiff
Use: hardy fuchsia, treat like other shrubs if planted in a bed

My tip: If possible, do not place pure white varieties in a sunny position, as they will tend to discolour.

4 "Hummeltje"

Raiser: Appel, 1979, Netherlands
Flower: single
Tube: light pink
Sepals: white pink
Corolla: light pink
Leaves: medium green, very small, round, dentate
Growth: bushy
Use: for pots, beds and hanging baskets. Also suitable for bonsai

5 "Happy"

Raiser: Tabraham, 1974, Britain
Flower: single
Tube: red
Sepals: red
Corolla: brilliant bluish-violet
Stamen: light red
Stigma: light red
Leaves: small, medium-dense foliage
Growth: upright, spherical, bushy
Use: equally suitable as a bedding or solitary plant. May also be trained for bonsai. Flowers are small but very numerous, directed slightly upward

"Vielliebchen", a hardy fuchsia.

"Alison Ewart" should not be placed in bright sunlight.

1 "Vielliebchen"

Raiser: Wolf, 1911, Germany
Flower: single
Tube: shiny red
Sepals: shiny red, narrow, slightly upright
Corolla: deep violet, with a red tinge towards the base
Stamen: red
Stigma: red
Leaves: medium sized, narrow
Growth: upright, bushy
Use: A very profusely flowering bedding plant, which is said to be hardy to a limited degree. It is especially suitable as a solitary plant and is good for use in bonsai

Some interesting facts about hardy fuchsias

Only choose varieties that are recommended by experts as being hardy or semi-hardy. Just like other shrubs, all hardy fuchsias will die down to ground level and start producing shoots from the ground again from the second month of spring.

Plant them in late spring, about 5-10 cm (2-4 in) deeper than usual.

From midwinter on, they should be protected against the cold by heaping a 15-cm (6 in) layer of leaves or peat around the plant.

2 "Alison Ewart"

Raiser: Roe, 1976, Britain
Flower: single
Tube: pink, short, thick
Sepals: pink with green tips
Corolla: pink, mauve
Stamen: pink
Stigma: light pink
Leaves: medium sized, dark green with red veins. Provide an attractive contrast to the flowers
Growth: upright, well branched
Use: equally suitable as a bush for tubs, containers, beds or as a solitary plant. In a sunny position the pink flowers will tend to bleach out. The flowers are early. Very suitable for an exhibition plant
NB: The mother plant is the attractive cultivar "Eleanor Leytham", and the father the fast-growing cultivar "Pink Darling". "Alison Ewart" has retained the stocky growth characteristic of the mother – without having inherited the mother's delicate constitution – and the very noticeable diagonal stance of the flowering stems and many flowers of the father plant.

Fuchsia flowers in the wild.

1 *Fuchsia boliviana var luxurians "Alba"*

Country of origin: Peru
Flower: single
Tube: brilliant white, long, slim
Sepals: brilliant light red, short, upright
Corolla: brilliant dark red
Stamen: red
Stigma: red
Leaves: very large, oval, slightly hairy
Growth: vigorous, does not form many branches
Use: best in a heated greenhouse or conservatory, where it will flower all winter as a climbing plant

2 *Fuchsia denticulata*

Country of origin: Peru, Bolivia
Flower: single
Tube: red, long
Sepals: red with greenish tips
Corolla: carmine red
Leaves: dark green, long, with reddish underside
Growth: upright and spindly
Use: as a solitary plant. It can stand sunlight and will flourish in a conservatory

3 *Fuchsia speciosa*

Hybrid, derived from *Fuchsia splendens x* and *Fuchsia fulgens*
Country of origin: Mexico

Flower: single
Tube: orange
Sepals: light orange with green tips
Corolla: light orange
Leaves: light green, hairy
Growth: upright
Use: bushes and standards. Also suitable for conservatories

4 *Fuchsia paniculata*

Country of origin: southern Mexico, Panama
Flower: single, shaped like a lilac spray
Tube: pinkish-red
Sepals: pinkish-red
Corolla: lavender blue
Leaves: medium green
Growth: upright, bushy
Use: solitary plant, also suitable for conservatories

5 *Fuchsia arborescens*

Country of origin: Central Mexico
Flower: single
Tube: rose red
Sepals: rose red
Corolla: violet pink
Flowers appear in sprays like lilac.
Leaves: large, long, elliptical, medium green, lighter undersides, reddish veins.
Growth: upright, bushy
Use: as a solitary plant
Position: sunny to semi-sunny
Speciality: will flower in a heated conservatory or greenhouse from mid-autumn until late spring

Fuchsia magellanica var. macrostemma (syn. var. gracilis)

Country of origin: Chile, Argentina
Flower: small, single
Tube: red
Sepals: red
Corolla: violet purple
Stamen: pink, protruding
Stigma: light red
Leaves: long, narrow, medium green
Growth: upright and graceful but with many shoots. Will grow to about 1 m tall (40 in)
Use: as a bedding plant, as it is hardy. Also as a solitary plant in containers but will then need frost-free winter quarters
NB: Nearly all fuchsias of the species *Fuchsia magellanica* are hardy. In a temperate climate they will behave like shrubs in winter, which means the parts above ground will die down and, in the spring, the plant will put out new shoots. During the following year, the root stock will increase and, as with shrubs, can be divided. This procedure should be repeated every four to six years.

Fuchsia magellanica var. macrostemma grows like a hardy shrub.

Useful information

International fuchsia societies

Australia
Australian Fuchsia Society
Box No 97
PO Norwood
South Australia 5067

Belgium
Les Amis du Fuchsia
rue de l'Espérance 62
4000 Liège

Britain
British Fuchsia Society
20 Bodawel
Llanon
Llanelli
Dyfed SA14 6BJ

Canada
British Columbia Fuchsia
and Begonia Society
2402 Swinburne Avenue
North Vancouver
British Columbia V7H 1L2

Denmark
Dansk Fuchsia Klub
V/Merete Printz
Frugtparken 1
2820 Gentofte

France
Section Fuchsia de la
SNHF
14 rue Brossement
Villeloy s/Yvette
Palaiseau 91120

Germany
Deutsche Fuchsien
Gesellschaft
674 Landau i.d. Pfalz
Den Altes Stadhaus
Koln

The Netherlands
Nederlandse Kring van
Fuchsia Vrienden
Graaf Floris V straat 6
Geertruidenberg

New Zealand
New Zealand Fuchsia
Society
PO Box 8843
Symonds Street
Auckland 1

Canterbury Horticultural
Society
Fuchsia Circle
25 Albert Terrace
St Martins
Christchurch 2

South Africa
South African Fuchsia
Society
Box 193
Hilton 3245
Natal

USA
American Fuchsia Society
Hall of Flowers
Garden Center of San
Francisco
Golden Gate Park
San Francisco
California 94122

National Fuchsia Society
6121 Monero Drive
Rancho Palos Verdes
California 90274

Zimbabwe
Fuchsia Society of
Zimbabwe
PO Box GD 115
Greendale
Harare

Preparing fuchsias for an exhibition or show

If you wish to exhibit especially beautiful specimens from your fuchsia collection, you will have to start your preparations months beforehand in order to bring your plants up to show standard:

● Cut back single flower varieties eight to ten weeks before the show date. In the case of double flowering plants, start 10 to 12 weeks beforehand.

● As soon as shoots appear, feed with a phosphorus-potassium based fertilizer. This will make the plant robust and resistant to disease and will encourage the development of many buds and flowers.

● Do not choose *triphylla* hybrids for garden shows in large halls as they quickly begin to drop their leaves. It is much better to choose single-flowering varieties, such as "Micky Goult" or "Joy Patmore".

● As far as double-flowering varieties are concerned, be careful that they do not open up too far, as they will then not survive transporting very well.

● Watch your plants' health during the preparation period before the show. For exhibition purposes they must be completely free of pests or disease.

When transporting exhibition plants, make sure that the transportation crates or boxes are well ventilated and do not allow excessive heat to accumulate. The root stocks must be kept moist but should not be freshly watered, and the parts of the plant above ground must be dry. Covering plants with polythene sheeting is not recommended.

After unloading at your destination, place the plants somewhere cool and shady.

Hybridizing
More and more fuchsia growers are now trying their hand at hybridizing. In addition to knowing the basics of Mendel's laws of inheritance the novice hybridizer will need a detailed knowledge of varieties in order to reach his or her goal within a reasonable time. He or she will also need some knowledge of the suitability of different species and varieties as "mother" or "father" plants. If you feel you lack knowledge, do not be discouraged as other hybridizers and your local fuchsia society will be pleased to help you.

"Winston Churchill"

Index

Figures given in bold indicate illustrations.

acid soil 18
anthers **8**
aphids **29**, 31
attic 37, 41

balcony 11, 13
  fuchsias for 12
  greenhouses 41
bark humus 17
baskets 24
  plastic 20
  wire 20
bastard cross 8
beds 11, 19, 20, 34
bonsai 25, 26
burn marks 28
bush fuchsias 13, 24, **39**
buying 14

Californian thrips **29**, 31
care 16, 38, 39
  mistakes in 28
caterpillars 30
chalky soil 18
chemical protection agents 28
colchicine 6
colour descriptions in catalogues 9
  range 12
compost 17, 18, 32
  ready-mixed 18
  to buy 18
  to mix yourself 18
composting box 37, 41
containers 17, 20
  plastic 17
  wooden 17
control of pests 26, 29-31, **29**
corolla 8, **8**
cultivars 60
cuttings 19, 32, **33**
  propagating from 32, **33**
  types of **33**
cyclamen mites 31

damage 28, **28**

dry 28
from light 28
mechanical 28
physiological 28
salt 28
decay of roots 29
deficiency, symptoms of 29
diseases 26-8
drainage 20

earth pit 35, **38**
electric light in winter 37
espaliers 25
evaporation, protection against 32, **32**
exhibitions 15, 60

fertilizer 18, 19. 20, 34, 39
  compound organic 19
  controlled-release 18, 19
  mineral compound 19
  regular 19
filaments 8, **8**
flowerhead 8
flowering time 14
flowers, colours of 9
  parts of **8**
  shapes of 8, **9**
foliage 9
frost 34
fruits 10
fuchsia, dessert sauce 11
  early flowering 41
  flan 11
  for balconies 12
  for bonsai 26
  hardy 11, 14
  indoor 12, 13, 14, 37
  preserve 11
  sun-loving 11, 13
  upright 12
  winter-flowering 11, 41
fungal diseases **28**, 29
fungicide 16, 26

gall midge 31
garden 13, 60
  centres 14
  soil 17

useful insects in 31
grafting 26, 32
greenhouse, lean-to 41
  mini 12
  plant protection agents 41
  subterranean 37
  useful insects in 31
grey mould 16, 23, **28**, 29
growing lamps 38
growth, cessation of 29
  vigorous 17

hanging baskets 13, 20, 22
  tying **19**
hanging plants 12, 16, **16**, 21, 24, 30
heating pipes, clay 38
herbal brews 26, 31
history of fuchsias 6
humidity 12
hybrids 6, 8
hydroculture 23
hydroponic system 22
hygrometer 40

insecticides 26
insects, useful 26, 31
internodal cuttings **33**
irrigation 22
  automatic 22

lacewing fly 31
layering 32, 34
leaves, colours of 9
  discoloured 28, 29
  falling 28
  shapes 9
  spots on 29
light shaft 37
lime 18
loam 18

mail order 14
mare's tail brew 26, 31
micro-climate 12
micro-nutrients 18
mildew **28**, 29
misting 13
mites, predatory 31

mulching 14
mutations 6

NPK 19
nurseries 14
nutrients 19

Onagraceae 8
ovary **8**
overwintering 14, 34, 38
  positions 35

patio 11, 13
peat, dark sedge 17
  light moss 17
petals 8, **8**
pH factor 17
phythium root decay 29
pinching out shoots **19**, 25
plant, solitary 20
planting in pots **18**, 33
  time 14, 15
plants, neighbouring 12, 13
  young 23, 25
polythene tunnel 41
position 11, 13
  improving 11
pots 13, 17, 19, 20
  clay 17
pricking out 33
propagating 32-4, **33**
  methods 32
protection agents, chemical 28
  of plants 31, 38, 41
pruning 22, 23, 39, 40
  before winter 34
  in speing 38
pyramid shape 25, 39

raiser 6
red spider mites 31
repotting 23, 34, 40
rhizoctonia 29
RHS 9
roots, decay of 29
rootstock, dividing the **39**
rust **28**, 29

sand 17

Index

sandy soil 18
seed 10, 32
sepals 8, **8**
shade 12
shapes, training into 10
shock from light **28**
shoots, propagating from **33**
shows 15, 60
shrubs 24
societies 60
soil 18
  improving 18
  loamy 18
spacing of plants 20
species 8
spider mites **29**, 31
sprays 26
stability 17
stairwells 37
stalks, decaying **8**
standards **5**, 13, 24, 25, **27**, **36**,
  38, 39
  in containers 12
  supports for **23**
  training **22**
stigma 8, **8**
stolons 32, 34
style 8, **8**
subspecies 8
sunlight, coping with 13
supports 25

tansy brew 28, 31
thrips 31
tidying 22
training fuchsias 24-6
transporting 16, 60
tube 8, **8**
tutor plant support 25

underplanting 12
unnatural growth of shoots 28

varieties 8, 16
varieties and cultivars
  "Achievement" 13
  "Alison Ewart" 57, **57**
  "American Prelude" **35**
  "Ann H. Tripp" 13

"Annabel" **3**, 13, 46, **46**
"Arcadia" **10**
"Architect L. Mercher" **cover**
"Beacon" **5**, **36**
"Beacon Rosa" **36**
"Blue Satin" **35**
"Brutus" **15**
"Cascade" **30**
"Chang" 13
"Cecile" **21**, 47, **47**
"Centrepiece" **35**
"Charming" **cover**, **7**
"Checkerboard" **15**
"Cliantha" 50, **50**
"Countess of Aberdeen" 53, **53**
"Covergirl" **15**
"Daisy Bell" 24, 52, **52**
"Dark Eyes" 46, **46**
"Delice" 44, **44**
"Deutsche Perle" **5**, **7**, 13
"Elfriede Ott" 12, 49, **49**
"First Success" 14
"Flying Cloud" 13
"Forget-Me-Not" 53, **53**
Fuchsia arborescens 7, 9, 14,
  58, **58**
Fuchsia boliviana var. luxurians
  "Alba" 58, **58**
Fuchsia denticulata 7, 9, 58,
  58
Fuchsia excorticata 7, 9
Fuchsia hartwegii **41**
Fuchsia lycioides 7
Fuchsia magdalenae 9
*Fuchsia magellanica var.
  macrostemma (syn. var.
  gracilis)* 6, 29, 59, **59**
Fuchsia microphylla 7, 9
Fuchsia paniculata 58, **58**
Fuchsia perscandens 7
Fuchsia procumbens 9
Fuchsia speciosa **3**, 14, 58, **58**
Fuchsia splendens 7
Fuchsia triphylla 6, 7
"Gartenmeister Bonstedt" **15**
"General Monk" 44, **44**
"Gesäuseperle" **48**, 49
"Göttingen" 13, 49, **49**
"Groenekan's Glorie" 13

"Happy" 12, 13, **16**, 26, 56, **56**
"Harry Gray" 12
"Hawkshead" 56, **56**
"Hilda" **cover**
"Hummeltje" 26, 56, **56**
"Joy Patmore" **2**, **7**, 13, 45, **45**
"Koralle" 13
"Kwintett" 8, 13, **36**
"La Campanella" 12, 13, 56, **56**
"Lady Isobel Barnet" **7**
"Lady Thumb" 12, 26
"Larissa" 12
"Leonhart von Fuchs" 54, **54**
"Liebreiz" 13
"Lisi" 12, 13
"Little Beauty" 13, 26, 44, **44**
"Lolita" 52, **52**
"Loni Jane" 50, **50**
"Lottie Hobby" 26
"Mantilla" **cover**
"Marcus Graham" **35**
"Margaret" **9**
"Miep Aalhuizen" 14
"Minirock" 26
"Minirose" 12
"Moonraker" **9**
"Mrs Lovell Swisher" **9**, 52, **52**
"Nettala" 54, **54**
"Orange Flare" 13
"Orange Mirage" **27**
"Parasol" 13
"Paula Jane" 44, **44**
"Pennine" 46, **46**
"Petit Point" **15**
"Pink Marshmallow" **35**
"Pink Quartett" 51, **51**
"Postiljon" 12
"Robert Stolz" 12
"Ron Ewart" 44, **44**
"Royal Velvet" **15**
"Satellite" **35**
"Sleigh Bells" **cover**, 13
"Small Pipes" **40**
"Son of Thumb" 56, **56**
"Southgate" 46, **46**
"Texas Longhorn" 16
"Thalia" 13
"Tinker Bell" 52, **52**
"Tom Thumb" 12, 13, 26

"Ullswater" **16**
"Vielliebchen **cover**, 26, 57, **57**
"Vobeglo" 55, **55**
"Walz" 13
"Wiebke Becker" 12
"Winston Churchill" **42**
"Wilsons Pearls" 44, **44**
ventilation 38
vine weevil 29

water balance 28
  hardness 22
  mains 22
  spring or well 22
watering 20, 22, 34, 38, 39
waterlogging 17, 26, 28
white fly **29**, 31
wild species 9
windbreak 12
winter garden 12, 13, 14, 37
  positions 35-7
  quarters 14, 34, 38

"Charming", a robust variety for beds or containers.

Cover photographs:
Front cover: *"Hilda"*
Inside front cover: *"Vielliebchen"*
Inside back cover: *"Charming"*
Back cover: *"Mantilla" (top left), "Sleigh Bells" (top right),*
"Architect L. Mercher" (below).

Photographic acknowledgements
Friedrich Strauss

This edition published 1994 by
Merehurst Limited
Ferry House, 51-57 Lacy Road,
Putney, London SW15 1PR
Reprinted 1995
© 1989 Gräfe und Unzer GmbH, Munich

ISBN 1 85391 390 1

A catalogue record for this book is available from the British Library.

English text copyright ©
Merehurst Limited 1994
Translated by Astrid Mick
Edited by Lesley Young
Design and typesetting by
Cooper Wilson Design
Illustrations by Ushie Dorner
Printed in Singapore by
Craft Print Pte Ltd